T0072579

Naked The Traveller

TRAVEL SMART!

TRAVEL MORE!

Peter Dolezal

Trafford
PUBLISHING®

*We at Trafford believe that it is the responsibility of us all, as both individuals
and corporations, to make choices that are environmentally and socially sound.
You, in turn, are supporting this responsible conduct each time you purchase a
Trafford book, or make use of our publishing services. To find out how you are
helping, please visit www.trafford.com/responsiblepublishing.html*

*Our mission is to efficiently provide the world's finest, most comprehensive
book publishing service, enabling every author to experience success.
To find out how to publish your book, your way, and have it available
worldwide, visit us online at www.trafford.com*

Trafford rev. 6/15/2009

www.trafford.com

North America & international
toll-free: 1 888 232 4444 (USA & Canada)
phone: 250 383 6864 ♦ fax: 250 383 6804
email: info@trafford.com

The United Kingdom & Europe
phone: +44 (0)1865 487 395 ♦ local rate: 0845 230 9601
facsimile: +44 (0)1865 481 507 ♦ email: info.uk@trafford.com

CONTENTS

Travel educates, energizes and entertains us. It challenges our senses, our attitudes, our abilities and often, our financial resources.

This is **not** another traveller's guide to Rome or Paris, or even to Italy or France. That role is very well fulfilled by the Rick Steves and Lonely Planet series, and countless other excellent destination-oriented publications which can be found in all book stores.

This is a traveller's handbook, written by a fellow traveller who has visited more than fifty countries on six continents, some on extensive business travel as CEO of several large corporations; many others for the simple joy of being a tourist with my wife.

Between us, there are few travel experiences, good and bad, which we have not encountered over the past thirty years. From these have flowed numerous lessons. It is my hope that other travellers - current or aspiring, can save needless headaches, time, and money, through the easy, and fun, reading of this guide.

Regardless of the objective of any given trip, careful planning to achieve best value has always been our objective.

The Naked Traveller identifies the *key issues associated with travel*. Each chapter provides insight into a specific topic, with many illustrative anecdotes. It delves into each issue, providing practical insights designed to minimize frustration and cost for the traveller, whether wealthy or of more modest means.

This guide offers as well, the added dimension of an appreciation, and even understanding, of various cultures. Between my wife Gaye and myself, we are able to bumble, stumble and even converse in some eight languages. Through this hard-learned, ever-evolving skill, we have gained insights into diversity, the world over. I hope to sensitize the reader to some of the cultural nuances to expect when travelling, in order to not offend and, ultimately, to be rewarded by a richer experience.

You may chuckle as you read on. The touch of humour, with a bit of spice thrown in, is usually at my expense!

So sit back; put your feet up. Prepare to absorb the many **TIPS** highlighted throughout the book. Useful and practical, they are based on numerous trips and many lessons learned. They should prove helpful as you plan your own adventures. Adopt them as your own, and apply them to all your travels.

The end result?

You will no longer be a ***naked traveller***, but rather, an astute, well-prepared individual ready to turn every travel opportunity into a thoroughly enjoyable, **best-value** experience.

YOUR OBJECTIVE:
- ***ENRICHED TRAVEL EXPERIENCES***
- ***REDUCED FRUSTRATION***
- ***GREATER VALUE FOR YOUR TRAVEL DOLLAR***

YOUR REWARD:
- ***MORE OPPORTUNITIES FOR TRAVEL***

CHAPTER ONE

THE TRAVEL CHOICES

Conquer Mount Kilimanjaro...Relive history on the beaches of Normandy...Marvel at nature in the Galapagos...Delight in the antics of Barbary monkeys in Gibraltar...Gaze in awe at architectural wonders world-wide...

Today's world is truly a pearl in the traveller's oyster. Travel opportunities are limited only by one's budget, schedule and health.

The first decision, even before selecting a target destination, is whether your objective is to travel:

- As cheaply as possible;
- At moderate cost; or
- First Class all the way.

Your budget category will impact greatly, the planning and booking strategies which you will follow.

Regardless of the weight of our wallet, we should always strive to obtain best-value for our travel-dollar. This book will assist you in meeting that objective.

. . . .

Your travel choices are as limitless as your imagination. Consider just some of the possibilities:

- Domestic vs. International travel
- Cruise options
- Air, Train or Bus travel
- Eco and Adventure holidays
- Hiking or Cycling holidays
- Resorts and All-Inclusive destinations
- Bed-and-Breakfast vs. Hotel accommodations
- Short getaways vs. Long-stay vacations
- Camping and RV-ing adventures
- Volunteering and Educational options.

Of course, a number of significant factors will impact your choices and strategies. For instance:

- Do you prefer travelling alone? With a partner? With family or friends?
- Is organized group travel for you? Or do you prefer independence?
- Do you have health issues or special needs?

Only *you* can select your destination, and the type of travel you prefer.

The scope of your budget, together with your age, health, *and* safety issues associated with various destinations, will help you to arrive at the right decision.

....

To initiate the planning process, list and debate the pros and cons of every option. Narrow your choices down to one or two. It's good to have a back-up plan. Your first choice may prove unavailable, too expensive, or otherwise impractical at this point in time.

Websites such as *www.youtube.com* provide unedited, first-hand *been there-done that* insights into destinations you may be considering.

....

You have selected your destination. Now is the time to become an *armchair traveller*. Begin your detailed research. Craft your best-value strategies, in preparation for booking your trip.

Last-minute travel bookings are almost always available, and can deliver spectacular value *if* you can take off on a few days' or weeks' notice. The reality however, is that until we retire, we must generally schedule vacations around our employment and/or our children's school obligations. This takes careful forethought and advance planning.

For your research and investigations, use every available resource. Scour the internet, travel ads, travel books and magazines and, not to be ignored, talk with your local travel agent. Friends, colleagues, and family have travel experiences to share. Pick their brains.

TIP # 1.... Effective planning and research is the first, and perhaps most important, step toward achieving best-value for your travel dollar, and to ensuring that you have a great holiday.

Before immersing yourself in detailed planning however, ensure that your holiday destination is affordable on *your* budget.

Be clear on both the source and availability of funds which will be needed.

Subsequent chapters provide an insight into the many practical strategies to use in achieving **best value** - whatever your budget, choice of destination, or means of travel.

. . . .

CHAPTER TWO

THE TRAVEL BUDGET

Rent the Hummer or the Volkswagen?...Book the Hot Air Balloon adventure or the walking tour?...Buy the Persian carpet or the baseball hat?...

Most of us must not only plan carefully, but also save, to afford our travels. No matter how economically you strive to travel, the cost will often exceed, by a significant amount, your normal at-home budget.

In developing a travel budget, keep in mind one important, often-forgotten source of funds.

Although there is no such thing as a free ride, one helpful contribution will make that ride somewhat easier.

Let's assume you plan to be away from home for two weeks.

Had you stayed home for those two weeks, you would have spent money on a daily basis. I'm not referring to mortgage, auto, utility and other fixed-payment obligations. These must continue whether you are at home or away.

However, your normal daily at-home spending on groceries, gas, entertainment, and other social activities, disappears when you are away on holidays. This amount is fairly easy to calculate.

From your household's total take-home pay, subtract *all fixed costs*, for the period you plan to be away. The residual balance will be the approximate amount that you can divert toward your holiday.

peter dolezal

If you are debt-free, as is often the case with retirees, this contribution to your holiday fund can be quite significant. This fact alone, enables many retirees living on limited incomes, to enjoy travel for as
long as their health permits.

*We know one retired couple, of very modest means, who have no debts.
They are able to relocate for five months every winter to Mexico. They
spend not a penny more there, than were they to stay home in snowy,
cold South Dakota! And this includes their airfare!*

More, in another chapter, on how, despite modest financial resources,
one can travel extensively.

TIP # 2..... **The lower your debt payments and other fixed
costs, the more affordable your next holiday; the
money you don't spend at home while away on
holiday, will contribute significantly to financing
the cost of your trip.**

You have been thinking about a trip for some time. Ideally, you
have been saving toward it before making an actual commitment.

Unfortunately, we live in a world of hype, advertising and enticement.
This often creates in many of us, a desire for instant gratification. We
want that new car, electronic toy, or trip to Hawaii, not in the future,
but NOW! North America's economic welfare largely depends in fact,
on this human trait.

Although I personally have never borrowed to travel, I do recognize
that borrowed funds finance many holidays in today's world.

If you *must* contemplate financing your trip in some manner, at least
do so as economically as possible.

Let's estimate a need for an additional $5,000 for our trip. This is over and above the $1,500 of daily at-home costs we will save by being away. This gives us a total budget of $6,500 for our two-week holiday. What, other than generous relatives, are our typical funding options for the extra $5,000?

1. ADD TO THE MORTGAGE

Your mortgage is up for renewal. You have substantial equity in your home. You have 20 years left on your mortgage, and your rate for the next five years will be fixed at 6%. It seems a no-brainer to simply add the $5,000 to the renewed mortgage amount.

Terrible idea! *Why?*

This seemingly minor $5,000 bump-up of your mortgage will add $35.61 per month to your payments. This seems quite reasonable and afford-able. However, over the remaining 20 years of your mortgage, assum-ing a constant 6% interest rate throughout, you will end up paying an extra $3,546 in interest, amounting to a total repayment of $8,546.

Remember too, your mortgage payments are made with *after-tax dol-lars*. If you are in a 40% marginal tax bracket during the subsequent 20 years, you must *earn* an extra $14,240, simply to pay off the $5,000 you initially borrowed for your travels!

Using this option would result in a very expensive trip! Just think of the extra holidays you could have had, by avoiding this high cost of borrowing, over the remaining life of your mortgage!

2. USE A CREDIT CARD

That's why we have a credit card, isn't it? Perhaps so. If your monthly cash flow is sufficient to repay a $5,000 charge to your card within a short period, say 12 months, the cost will be tolerable. At a mini-mum 18% credit card interest rate, you will have paid back, at $461 per month, about $5,532. The additional premium of $532 may be a reasonable price for that holiday you *really* need now.

However, if you are among those credit card users whose monthly payments rarely exceed the minimum monthly amounts payable, you could be repaying the $5,000 over many years, and at a cost which is even greater than the mortgage-financing option.

3. LINE OF CREDIT

If you *must* borrow for your trip, a line of credit, often secured by the equity in your home, is probably overall, your least expensive source of funds. Typically, the interest rate will be set at around prime.

Using 6% as our prime rate, the $5,000 borrowed on a line of credit would, if repaid within one year, incur about $164 in interest costs. If three years were required to repay the loan, your interest costs would total a still-modest $580, a significant improvement over the other borrowing options.

....

One fact to consider: If this year's trip has been financed with *borrowed funds*, your repayment obligations may limit or delay your ability to take another holiday, until after you have repaid the first loan.

Clearly, if at all possible:

- *Plan* for your holiday;
- *Work* up a budget;
- *Save* for it in advance.

Then, book and enjoy your trip, without the pain of a debt facing you upon your return home.

One easy, relatively painless way to make a significant contribution to your travel fund, is to throw all the change you have in your purse or wallet at the end of each day, into a large jar, coffee can, or piggy bank. Despite the hassle this may cause you in eventually rolling up this mass of coinage, you may discover that, over a year, you have effortlessly managed to save more than $1,000!

TIP # 3 ..... Do your best to pay for a trip from savings. If you *must* borrow to finance your travel, use the cheapest means available. *Never, ever,* increase your mortgage amount to pay for a holiday!

....

You have planned and worked out your $6,500 vacation budget. You know *how* you will pay for your holiday.

Your challenge now, is to:

- Ensure that the destination you have in mind fits that budget, and, most important,
- Achieve **best-possible value for those travel-dollars.**

You are now ready to begin the detailed work of planning and booking your trip.

Your reward? Greater travel value for your hard-earned travel dollar.

. . . .

CHAPTER THREE

WHEN TO TRAVEL

The school calendar, business and work commitments, or other obligations usually dictate when you can travel. This may force you into expensive, high-season holidays such as Christmas, Spring Break, or during the summer months.

BUT.....

If you have the flexibility, be smart in your choices, to achieve **best value** for your travel dollar.

Numerous destinations, such as the French Riviera, Portugal's Algarve, and other Mediterranean locales have a comfortable climate during the off-season winter months. They can be enjoyed at a fraction of their high-season cost.

Mexico, the Caribbean, and Central and South America offer similar opportunities for bargains *if* you are willing to visit during the off-season, or even in the fringe, shoulder-seasons.

TIP # 4 ..... Never assume that dream-come-true destinations are out of reach of your travel budget. Check out the values available in fringe season or off-season periods.

One of the best websites for exploring different destinations, and the best months for a visit, is *www.besttimetogo.com*. This site offers temperature and rainfall information, for each month of the year, for major destinations world-wide.

Referring to this site, my wife and I researched a February trip to the Amazon basin. We knew to expect about 225 mm of rain, with average temperature highs of 31 degrees Celsius. This information proved to be quite accurate; it was indeed, wet and hot, but fore-warned, we were properly outfitted.

This website, a great resource for the traveller, also provides basic information on the *average* daily cost of a visit, although I find it to be on the high side, more reflective of the costs incurred by a neophyte traveller. On the plus side, the site also features useful maps, details on food choices, and much more.

If you *do* choose to become an off-season bargain hunter, remember there *is* a reason why fewer people visit specific destinations at certain times of the year. These reasons often relate to weather. Be sure you are willing to accept the conditions that make others stay away.

If this is not an issue for you, you will find that airlines, hotels, and re-sorts will be tripping over themselves to offer special deals to attract you, often at almost unbelievable, reduced prices.

Winter resorts for instance, such as Whistler in Canada, and Aspen in the U.S., often cut their rates significantly in the non-skiing periods, offering great hiking, cycling, golf, and numerous other vacation ac-tivities during the off-season.

Many countries in Europe are no joy for the high-season summer vis-itor. Tour buses and rental cars clog the roads. Countless tourists, many of them holidaying urbanites, swarm the charming towns and popular sites. Long lineups await entrance to museums and other at-tractions. Those in the travel and service industries may well be short on patience.

By mid-to-late September however, children are back to school, holi-days are generally over for the local populace, and the weather is still great! Hotel and restaurant prices start dropping.

Your spring, autumn, and even winter, visit will not only be less expensive, but also more relaxed and enjoyable!

Travel in September, October, or November, to southern hemisphere continents can also work to your advantage. It's spring-time in Australia, Africa and South America - pleasant and, because it is off-season, less expensive.

TIP # 5..... **Fringe-season and off-season travel can be very enjoyable, and can represent superb value. Do your homework however, before booking. Clearly understand, and accept, the circumstances which cause some travellers to stay away during the same period when you are planning to visit.**

CHAPTER FOUR

REWARD - TRAVEL

An effective way to significantly reduce trip costs, is to book your airfare using accumulated reward travel miles. Before you do this however, here are a few points to keep in mind when using these reward plans.

1. THE REWARD-TRAVEL PLAN

a) It costs nothing to join an airline's reward plan. Whether you travel often, or only occasionally, every flight you take on that airline will earn you reward miles.

Most airlines with reward-travel incentives have, among their many affiliations, partnerships with other airlines. Become familiar with their list of partners. Always provide your membership number if you happen to book with a partner.

b) The other important vehicle for amassing reward miles, is the credit card, on which your spending earns travel miles. Choose a card that accumulates miles in the reward plan which you most prefer.

Choose the specific credit card with care. Do not be afraid to pay a somewhat higher annual membership fee if a premium card offers you 50 to 100% more reward miles, than does a basic card. The extra $25 or $50 in annual fees may be well worthwhile if you plan to travel extensively.

Limit yourself to only one or two credit cards, so that your reward miles accumulation is concentrated on one or two travel plans. If you have multiple cards, and your spending is spread across all of them, no one reward plan will benefit you by very much.

c) Be conscious of the rewards affiliations of many businesses in both the tourism and retail sectors. Booking with specific hotel chains and resorts, or car rental companies for instance, will often result in the addition of reward-miles to your primary reward collection plan. If the basic price on several options is similar, go with the establishment that earns you reward miles.

Nothing beats the value of miles accumulated, simply as the result of your normal expenditures.

When negotiating very competitive renewal terms on her mortgage, our daughter was delighted to learn that for each dollar of monthly payments during her new five-year term, she would earn an equivalent number of reward miles in her major travel plan.

TIP # 6..... Try to concentrate your travel-miles accumulation on one or two plans only.

---

2. ACCELERATED ACCUMULATION OF REWARD-MILES

a) Some financial institutions may offer huge initial reward-miles incentives to entice you to sign up for a specific credit card. These bonuses can be as high as 20,000 reward-miles, with on occasion, the added bonus of a "Partner Travel" discount certificate. Some plans even award a new discount coupon annually!

Our daughter and her family recently flew from Vancouver to Los Angeles. With the bonus discount coupon, her partner was able to fly, there and back, for $50 plus taxes.

The savings on that one trip paid the annual credit card fee for four or five years!

b) If you book airfare and/or accommodation using your airline-partner credit card, the bonus reward-miles you earn for the trip are occasionally increased, even doubled! This is in addition to the reward-miles you will already earn, simply by using the credit card in the first place.

c) If you travel frequently on business for your employer, check company policy regarding travel. If the policy permits, use your personal credit card to pay for your airfares, accommodation and other related business expenses; recover the cost on your expense account.

If you *are* able to do this, be sure however, to pay off the balance before interest charges accumulate! This requires discipline. If you can do this successfully, you will add significantly to your reward miles account, at no extra cost.

Employers are often quite amenable. It's a small reward for you, at no cost to them, for all the travel you do on their behalf! Of course, if you are the business owner, you can ensure that all of your business expenses are charged to the card of your choice. You will earn reward-miles quickly.

d) On occasion, an aging parent or someone else to whom you are close, no longer needs, wants, or plans to redeem accrued reward-miles. Most plans permit redemption of those miles either for a ticket in your name, or a transfer to your account, for a reasonable fee.

One major plan, for example, permits you to purchase miles from any other account-holder, for two cents a mile. You may find this to be good value. Not only does such a transfer allow you to top up the reward-miles in your account, but also, those hard-earned reward-miles will not go to waste by being cancelled.

TIP # 7 ..... Use every technique your reward-travel account permits, to increase its miles value more quickly.

- You will be able to travel sooner, and/or further, on your travel-reward plan.
- The value of your reward-miles is one of the few tax-free benefits you can still receive!

3. VALUE OF REWARD-MILES

Accounting rules require that corporations offering reward plans record a *contingent liability* on their balance sheet, for outstanding reward-miles which people like you and I hold, and which can be redeemed at a future date. To minimize this exposure, they try to reduce their liability in a number of ways. Be aware of the practices that result from this, and their potential consequences.

a) With some plans, you will lose *all* the reward-miles you have accumulated in your account, if you have had no account activity for as little as one year. Often the only account activity required, is to accumulate a few more reward-miles by using the appropriate credit card on a purchase, even a very minor one.

We recently learned that our substantial balance of reward-miles with a European carrier will expire in the next year. Before the year is up, we plan to book a flight to a European destination which we have always planned to visit. If necessary we will, within the allowable subsequent twelve months, pay a small fee to change the specific date to a more convenient one. Using this technique, we will gain an extra year in which to actually redeem those reward-miles.

b) Many frequent-flyer reward plans increasingly try to entice members to redeem reward-miles for other than free flights. You are offered services, or items ranging from toasters to bicycles to large-screen televisions. Free accommodation at various hotel chains, and car rentals from a range of agencies are also offered.

Let's examine a few offerings. Compare the **dollar-value** we receive for these reward-mile redemptions, to the value of accumulating them for air tickets. The following are taken directly from a current on-line redemption site for a major North American plan:

- **$50** Callaway Golf Umbrella **(5,000 reward-miles)** - Value/Mile: **1.00 cent**

- **$100** Future Shop Gift Card **(13,000 reward-miles)** - Value/Mile: **0.77 cent**

- **$2,500** Vespa LX50 Scooter **(627,000 reward-miles)** - Value/Mile: **0.40 cent**

This random sample of redemption options demonstrates that, in terms of dollar-value, one receives at most, *one cent for each mile redeemed.* As the retail value of the item increases, the value of each reward-mile decreases!

Imagine on the other hand, how far one could travel on the same 627,000 reward-miles that are required for a $2,500 scooter! On many carriers, this number of reward-miles could net you as many as six round-trip Business Class tickets, almost anywhere in the world.

c) If one travels frequently by air, there is no better use for reward-miles than air travel. Without exception, I have found this to produce the greatest benefit, **particularly if I plan my miles redemptions for Business Class flights.**

To illustrate:

Air travel reward-plans want you to *use up* as quickly as possible, even a modest balance of reward-miles in your account. As a result, they often offer short-haul economy flights for as little as 20,000 reward-miles.

If you determine the real dollar-cost of such a flight, you actually save very little, compared to the value of accumulating those same reward-miles for a longer, much more expensive, flight.

....

The following table provides a specific example. Listed are a sampling of a major plan's redemption requirements, along with its posted dollar-cost for the identical roundtrip fare, for three separate destinations: two in Canada and one in Australia.

Departure	Destination	Miles Required Economy	Dollar Cost Economy	Value Per Point	Miles Required Business	Dollar Cost Business	Value Per Point
Victoria BC	Edmonton Alberta	15,000	$337	2.25 cents	N/A	N/A	N/A
Victoria BC	Moncton NB	25,000	$1,190	4.76 cents	40,000	$4,358	10.9 cents
Victoria BC	Sydney Australia	75,000	$1,842	2.46 cents	100,000	$12,400	12.4 cents

This, and the previous table, demonstrate that even the cheapest short-haul economy flight in North America, redeemed at 2.25 cents per mile, represents two to five times greater value, than redeeming those same reward-miles to acquire merchandise or services.

Furthermore, the tables demonstrate that **if you have the patience** to wait, and to accumulate enough reward-miles for redemption for Business Class tickets on a long-haul trip, such as to Australia, your economic value per reward-mile will be up to fifty times greater, than if redeemed for merchandise or services!

Keep in mind that as fuel prices trend higher, mileage plans will undoubtedly increase the number of reward-miles required for free air travel. If you are fortunate enough to have accumulated a large balance, it may be wise to redeem some miles at current require-ment levels, rather than risk their value eroding.

....

All of the above examples are direct offerings from *one* reward-mile plan. You will find however, that the principles outlined will be quite similar with most plans. For all reward programs to which you belong, do your own calculations. Make sure that you are redeeming miles in a manner which provides **best value** for your particular circumstance.

TIP # 8 ..... The best-value redemption of miles in rewards programs, is almost always for free air travel, rather than for merchandise or services. Mileage redemptions for Business Class travel deliver by far, the greatest value.

---

4. REDEEMING REWARD-MILES FOR FLIGHTS

You have now accumulated enough reward-miles for a trip-for-two to Hawaii. You want to redeem them for two Business Class tickets. It's six months before you plan to travel. You decide to book your reward travel on-line.

Frustration! The only available pair of tickets, for the approximate dates you want, will cost you more than 300,000 reward miles, rather than the posted 120,000. *Why is this so?*

Unfortunately, in this instance, you have left your booking too late, particularly for Business Class seats. Airlines allocate very few reward-seats per plane. Usually, they allot no more than 6 to 8% of seats in Economy, and even fewer in Business Class, at their normal redemption value. Most plans don't want to deny the traveller outright. Instead, they will offer extra seats, but at a much higher mileage-redemption cost. If you speak to a *real person* at the particular reward-plan office, you will be told that the premium miles are charged because "extra" reward-seats are purchased by the reward-plan, from the airline, at normal retail prices.

....

Not having enough *extra* reward-miles - or simply refusing to "*pay*" the higher premium - you try the 1-800 number for the airline.

You will probably find that, by shifting your travel dates a little, you can book two *Economy Class* tickets for the posted 80,000 reward-miles. This is not what you had planned on. You're somewhat disappointed, but that is the compromise you end up accepting as your "*free*" flight.

Remember too, few such flights are in fact *free*. Taxes and various government and airport fees which you are required to pay, may well add up to more than $100 per ticket.

While it will cost you extra, perhaps another $30, to book your reward-travel, it is often worthwhile to talk directly to a Plan agent. They often have access to reward-seats before they register on their website; they can also access their Partner-Reward travel options. This is particularly useful if you are trying to book Business Class travel at the posted rewards-redemption level.

TIP # 9 ..... **In order to greatly increase your chances of redeeming reward-miles for the tickets you want, particularly in hard-to-get Executive Class, be prepared to make your booking up to twelve months before your planned travel.**

Airlines release reward seats no earlier than about a year prior to your desired flight date. Many do not release until approximately six months in advance. It's best to call the Reward Plan 1-800 number to determine the precise advance release date for the airline in which you are interested. Mark your calendar. Be ready to try online, or call the Reward Plan, on the exact seat opening date, particularly for coveted Business Class travel.

I've even gone so far, when different time zones are involved, to set my alarm for just before 5:00 a.m. Pacific-time, in order to start dialing the Plan's 1-800 number on the dot of the 8:00 a.m. Eastern-time opening hour on the appropriate date.

....

Some reward plans have eliminated this issue for the traveller, by converting reward-miles to **travel vouchers** for specific dollar values. These vouchers can be applied directly to the cost of any available seat on many airlines. You make the booking in exactly the same manner you normally would. In this case however, you can offset part, or possibly all, of the cost with your voucher.

This alternative voucher-reward plan can be very good value for the traveller. This is particularly so, if your travel tends to be shorter, less expensive routes, and you are content to travel in Economy Class. Given the high retail cost of a Business Class ticket, your voucher will generally cover too little of the premium demanded.

TIP # 10 ..... **To optimize your booking flexibility, consider reward plans which allow you to redeem points for cash vouchers, which can then be applied to the cost of your ticket.**

A valuable *bonus* benefit of most reward-travel plans is that for a modest fee of $25 to $50, you can usually modify or cancel your planned travel, right up to the day of departure. Even should you cancel, you will not lose your reward-miles. They will be returned to your account for future redemption. This is a very welcome feature, which *may* save you the need to purchase Trip Cancellation Insurance.

CHAPTER FIVE

PURCHASED AIR TRAVEL

You don't have enough reward-miles for your next trip. You have no choice but to join the throng and go shopping for the best deal available.

A useful website with which to start your search is one with the rather unusual name, ***www.itasoftware.com***. It provides a terrific overview of fare and route options between any two locations, world-wide. This site however, does not list flights on many low-cost airlines.

Before finalizing your booking, check out at least these additional websites:

- ***www.wegolo.com*** for discount carriers;
- ***www.whichbudget.com*** for options among national carriers;
- ***www.hotwire.com*** which may offer the lowest price; however it will reveal the specific carrier and exact schedule only *after* you have booked and paid for the flight.

Better known, and also useful, sites for comparisons are ***www.expedia.com***; ***www.orbitz.com***; and ***www.travelocity.com***. In my experience however, they do not deliver as significant a value as those listed above.

There are no hard and fast rules governing *when to book for best-value*. But a few specific approaches are worth considering:

1. BOOKING EARLY

When airlines first open bookings for a specific flight, that is when they will usually offer the best fares. As the flight substantially sells out, ticket prices will tend to increase.

Last April, our daughter and her family knew they wanted to return to Mexico the following February. Planning their travel budget, they researched the fares for their preferred dates, on a major carrier's route from Vancouver to Zihuatanejo. The round-trip tickets were quoted at approximately $500 per person. By the time they actually made an on-line booking in August, for exactly the same dates and flights, the cost had risen to around $800 per person.

In this case, their delay in purchasing their three tickets cost them an additional $900.

TIP # 11 ..... Planning a trip well in advance, and booking early, will often save you significantly, on your flight costs.

---

2. BOOKING "LAST-MINUTE"

A seeming contradiction to the early-booking option above, is the fact that a truly last-minute booking—perhaps within a week of departure - **may** get you a jaw-dropping deal. It costs the airline very little more, to fly a plane that is 100%, rather than 90%, full. As a result, the airline may drop its price dramatically, to fill those last few seats. Other than the additional fuel cost, every extra dollar of revenue on those last few seats, is profit for the airline.

Google *Last Minute Travel* to find a multitude of options in which to explore a possible deal.

Of course, there is a catch! To take advantage of these deep discounts, your schedule must be highly flexible. Great for retirees or students, but not for the majority of us who, to accommodate other obligations, must depart and return on very specific dates.

TIP # 12....Last-minute travel may result in significant savings, if your schedule provides the necessary flexibility, and more so, if you are open to alternative destinations.

Stand-by travel, once the ultimate form of economical last-minute travel, is no longer easily found. Yes, you can arrive at an airport and try to fly stand-by. However, this option exists primarily for those who have missed an earlier flight, or for emergencies, for those who really must travel at the last moment. The ticket agent will sell you a seat, if one is available, but you are unlikely to get a discount.

In some countries, particularly those with still-developing economies, the old form of stand-by travel is still available. Do check before booking, just in case!

3. SHOPPING AROUND AMONG CARRIERS

Almost every household in North America owns a computer, or has easy access to one at their public library. The on-line information network provides tremendous flexibility for price-shopping between carriers, and various discounters.

A few extra minutes of research and comparison-shopping may save you significantly on the cost of your ticket. It probably matters little, through whom you buy your ticket, or which carrier you use, as long as they can meet your schedule needs, at the best price.

In addition to the websites listed earlier, another useful site is ***www. insidetrip.com***, which provides the typical airline price-options to your destination. Additionally however, it also rates each option - report card-style, on a scale of 1 to 100. The scores measure a combination of price, comfort, on-time performance, and number of stops for the various alternatives. This added information allows the traveller to obtain an insight into more than just the price differences, in order to make a true, best-value choice.

You may be very happy to pay an extra $50 for a ticket on a carrier with more leg room, and fewer enroute stops, than to choose the cheapest option.

4. BOOKING THE FLIGHT

You have finally settled on the best-value option that fits both your schedule and your travel budget. You found it directly on the airline's website.

It is usually best to try to make the reservation yourself, on-line. If you are determined instead on establishing phone contact with an airline agent, you are likely to be charged an extra $25 or more, *per ticket*, for the privilege. Employees cost airlines money; you are paying their salary.

You may instead, prefer to book your flight through a travel agent. That agent *may* well charge you a booking fee. As a cost-saving measure, many airlines have discontinued the practice of paying commissions to agents, especially on domestic flights.

Your travel agent may choose to waive this fee, if the specific flight is part of a larger, comprehensive holiday-package which you are booking. It's best to ask about fee schedules at the outset, so that you are not later surprised.

If your schedule permits, consider booking flights that depart on a

Tuesday, Wednesday, Saturday, or a holiday. Flights on these days tend to be less crowded and hence, often less expensive.

> **TIP # 13.....** An extra thirty minutes searching various websites may save you hundreds of dollars in airfare, and provide you with an overall better-value trip. This is one of the easiest ways to stretch your travel budget.

5. BOOKING THE BEST SEATS

Before booking your seats, you may wish to check ***www.seatguru. com.*** Study the seat configuration on the aircraft you will be flying. The site will tell you which seats have the most leg and elbow room, and as importantly, which seats to absolutely avoid. Who actually *wants* to sit next to the toilets with their constant traffic?

> **TIP # 14.....** Avoid surprises. Always confirm flight times prior to departure. Flights do get changed, delayed and cancelled.

CHAPTER SIX

UPGRADING TO BUSINESS CLASS

*Who among us, walking through the Business or Execu-
tive Class section, on our way to the back of the plane, has
not been envious of the sixteen or so travellers comfortably ensconced in their spacious armchair seats, awaiting personalized service, free beverages and a hot meal
shortly after take-off? I know I have. The longer the flight,
the more envious I am!*

Wishful as we are, we either cannot afford the generally huge premium
required for the extra comfort, or we simply refuse to "shell out".

Are we therefore always destined to fly Economy? Or are there strategies we can use, to obtain that magic upgrade, at a reasonable price,
or even better, for free?

1. REWARD - TRAVEL BOOKING

To recap, Chapter Four demonstrated that booking Business Class
travel, through reward-mileage redemption, provides the best-value
reward option for the traveller. The greatest value was realized in
booking long-haul flights to distant destinations such as Australia,
Asia, or South America.

Keep that fact in mind as you accumulate your reward miles. Consider delaying their redemption until you have collected the 75,000 or
100,000 miles required for each long-haul ticket.

We have flown Business Class to Australia, with a ten-day stopover in Hawaii. We have also flown Business Class to South Africa, with a Hong Kong stopover. Another trip, again Business Class, took us to Rio de Janeiro in Brazil. Each of these otherwise costly flights was made possible because we have always managed to resist using our accumulated reward-mileage for anything other than long-haul tickets.

2. REWARD - TRAVEL UPGRADES

Some reward-travel programs, upon *purchase* of Economy Class tickets, will permit you to redeem as few as 10,000 reward-miles, per ticket, to upgrade to Business Class. Even with limited accrued miles in your account, such an option may provide you the opportunity to enjoy Business Class travel, at Economy-class prices.

3. LAST - MINUTE UPGRADE PURCHASE

Some airlines permit purchase of an upgrade to Business Class, within 24 hours of your scheduled flight, for as little as $100 per seat, subject to availability. You *may* even be able to do so at the last minute, at the check-in counter, *if* seats are available.

Airlines are usually more than happy to fill the more expensive seats, since the greater demand is for the cheaper ones in Economy class. In the final analysis, this allows the airline to fill more seats on the plane, while still receiving a small premium for the seat upgrades. It's good business for the airline's bottom line.

And for you, upgrading to the comfort of Business Class, at such a modest cost, is a bargain!

4. CHARTER - AIRLINE BUSINESS CLASS

Some charter air carriers provide only an Economy class seating arrangement throughout the plane.

In recent years however, many have begun offering a small "Preferred", "Premium Economy", and even a Business Class section. Although these options may not be as lavish as you will find on major scheduled airlines, they do offer larger seats and more leg room. The cost of an upgrade in this circumstance, may be a modest premium of $200 to $300, as opposed to the usual premium of thousands of dollars.

On a charter flight to Europe, we booked Premium Economy seats. The fare for our very comfortable flight ended up within about $100 of the best regular Economy class fare for the same dates, with a major, scheduled carrier.

Occasionally, major international carriers on long-haul routes, particularly for travel between North America and Asia, will advertise very attractive prices for Business Class seats. These special, often short-term promotions, aim to attract the business traveller, or promote a new route or schedule.

Check around. Know your options *before* making that all-important booking. You *may* be pleasantly surprised.

TIP # 15 ..... **Don't assume that Business Class travel is automatically unaffordable or not worthwhile. Check all the possibilities. You may find an exceptional deal that invites you to indulge yourself.**

---

5. THE BEGGING SYSTEM

Strange as it seems, begging can work. It has for us, on at least a dozen occasions. I hesitate to share this with so many; if everyone tries it, my odds of future success will lessen dramatically! But since you paid for this book, I will 'fess up!

a) As a frequent flyer, flashing your airline program's "Elite" or "Super Elite" status card, or its equivalent, used to be a sure bet for a free upgrade if a seat was available. No longer as simple today, it *can*, on occasion still work.

If the airline is oversold in its Economy Class, some passengers are often invited to move up to available Business Class seats, in order to fill more seats on the plane. In that instance, the air carrier will first attempt to *move up* its most loyal reward-plan members on that flight.

If you are a "frequent flyer" who earns reward-miles more through actual flights than with credit card activity, you will enjoy a higher-status consideration, which can prove helpful in securing an upgrade.

Although most airlines' computers now track the frequent-flyer status of their passengers, I continue to make it a practice to always politely express my interest in a possible upgrade. I present my membership card, at both the check-in counter, and again at the boarding gate.

Always be polite and low-key! Aggressive or pushy behaviour will rarely achieve the objective. Simply smile and indicate your gratitude for being considered, if an opportunity arises.

My wife and I have, several times, enjoyed the unexpected last-minute thrill of being upgraded on our way to or from Europe. On one long flight to Australia, we were upgraded even further, from Business to the superior luxury of First Class!

b) Arrive early at the check-in counter, when the agent is not yet too rushed. Even if you have limited, or no, reward-travel miles on that airline, it costs nothing to ask if there is a possibility that they may need to upgrade passengers if Economy Class is overbooked. Politely, make it clear that you would be more than delighted to help them out!

*Once, while checking in for a Czech Airlines flight out of Prague, I did exactly that. To my amazement, the agent smiled and immediately upgraded us to Business Class. Clearly, she was aware that Economy class was oversold on that flight. We were either the first to check in, or the first to ask! Of course, it **may** have helped that I was a Canadian who conversed in fluent Czech with the agent!*

Recognize that although this approach is a long-shot, it does, on occasion, work.

....

During all of these "begging" antics in which I regularly engage, my wife tends to edge away, pretending to not know me. But when my approach works, she has yet to refuse the upgrade!

In most cases, your best bet will be to redeem your reward-miles, or to purchase a discount airline's bargain Business Class ticket that may cost little more than the Economy fare on other carriers.

Do, however, keep the other approaches in mind. Try them out, very politely and with a smile. You never know, you may succeed; but not if you don't try!

TIP # 16 ..... Shop for Business Class bargains. Actively seek out upgrading possibilities whenever you travel long distances.

∙∙

CHAPTER SEVEN

TRAVEL PASSES—Air, Train & Bus

Significant budget-stretchers for independent travellers of all ages, throughout many areas of the world, are a variety of passes for extended travel by air, train or bus.

It is easy, as part of your trip-planning process, to educate yourself on the various options available. Simply google for example, ***Australian Air Passes***. You will find all the information you need, including prices for the options offered. The same applies to train and bus travel in most countries.

In many cases these passes must be purchased **prior to departure** from your home country.

1. AIR PASSES

Last-minute bookings of individual point-to-point flight segments, once within your destination country, can be very expensive. Instead, check out ***www.airtimetable.com/airpass.htm***. You will often find a far more economical solution.

Read the fine print carefully. Aside from saving you money, the one thing which most of these passes have in common, is that they *must* be purchased at the same time you book your original flight *to* that country or continent.

The *ultimate in air passes*, for the encumbrance-free graduate, or the retiree with a wealth of available time and resources, is the "round-the-world" air pass. Again, in searching the web, you will find literally hundreds of options, from a low of about $1,200 for the ultimate budget trip, to a one-year, 38,000-mile Business Class ticket, for about $15,000!

When you consider that one can pay $12,000 for a single round-trip Business Class ticket between North America and Australia, you can easily see the tremendous value and appeal of the above options. The cost of these passes will normally reflect the overall total mileage you wish to fly, and the number of continents you wish to visit.

Many rules govern the use of such passes, the most significant being that *usually*, you can not backtrack. Generally, you must continue in either an easterly or westerly direction. Prices can increase if you cross over or zigzag between the northern and southern hemispheres.

Some round-the-world passes *include* the bonus of extra flights within each continent. You can stay for as long as you wish at each stop-over, subject to the overall time limit, usually twelve months, for your entire trip. This gives you the freedom to create an itinerary tailor-made to your specifications, and to reserve specific flights as and when you choose.

Air passes can result in substantial savings, particularly when extensive long-distance travel is involved. They are worth checking out in some detail.

2. TRAIN PASSES

Train passes are available on most continents. Google ***Train Passes*** for many options.

The U.S. has its **Amtrak USA Rail Pass**, and Canada, its **VIA Rail CanRail Pass**.

Perhaps the best known is Europe's **Eurail Pass**, which *must* be purchased in North America, *before* your departure, either on-line or through your travel agent. It is not available for purchase once you arrive in Europe.

This pass entitles you to First-Class train travel, including passage on some European ferry systems. From a long list, you choose the specific country, or network of countries, through which you wish to travel. The pass is available for different combinations: number of days, number of countries, and the overall period during which it is in effect. Travel dates and times, within the chosen parameters, can be selected and if desired, reserved, once you are in Europe. Although specific seat reservations are not always necessary, they are a good idea if your travel is on popular routes, or in high season. The few extra euros you pay for reserved seats on an overnight train, may save you the cost of a hotel, or at worst, an uncomfortable journey, if the train happens to be full.

A young friend and her new husband delayed their honeymoon while saving for an extensive backpacking trip by train through Europe. Armed with their crisp, new Eurail pass, they arrived by air in Frankfurt and headed directly to an overnight train for the first leg of their journey. They spent that whole long night sitting on their bags, in the cramped and noisy train corridor. It was back-to-school week in early September; every seat was occupied.

Seat reservations, had they known, could have been pre-booked, and would have saved them a very uncomfortable start to their holiday.

Although this will occur very rarely, you may occasionally travel on a train with second-class cars only. You will receive no partial rebate on your pre-purchased First Class Eurail Pass. Be assured, almost all trains on major routes have First Class cars.

Seniors travelling together, with for example, a Flexi-Pass, qualify for a reduced rate. From ages 12 to 25, travellers qualify for a "youth" or student discount, for second-class travel only. Further discounts are offered for children under 12.

Otherwise, if you are 26 years of age or older, your only option is to purchase a First-Class pass. This cost, however, can still be as much as 50% less than the cost of a series of regular-price, Second Class tickets, purchased in Europe, for the same destinations.

Keep in mind that the Eurail Pass is a valuable legal document, and is almost impossible to replace if lost.

Read the fine print regarding the exact manner of initial validation.

Sadly, we once observed a young couple on our train being denied their pre-paid passage because they had failed to properly validate their pass. Unable to use their pass until they could subsequently validate it, they had no recourse but to purchase new tickets for that leg of their journey.

One of the best insights into Eurail Passes can be found at **_www.ricksteves.com_**. This site not only orients you to all the options available, but also allows you to purchase your pass online.

TIP # 17..... Eurail passes are a superb way to travel both economically and comfortably by train in Europe. However, you must purchase these passes before leaving North America.

Train passes usually do save you money, when compared to the normal point-to-point fares in your destination country. But take note! *If* your objective is to travel in the *cheapest* manner possible, train passes, despite their discounts, may not be the best option.

A number of no-frills discount airlines may fly you quickly, point-to-point, throughout Europe, for less than the cost of a train pass. These flights can be effective budget-stretchers where necessary, but they come at the considerable sacrifice of missing the pleasures of the countryside you can enjoy from a train.

Read the fine print on specific discount flights. Be sure that after the added costs for luggage, taxes, and other fees are factored in, your flight really *is* a bargain.

....

Train travel throughout many of Europe's former eastern-block countries is still extremely affordable at regular point-to-point prices. For now, train passes for those countries are therefore less beneficial or necessary.

The advantages of travel by train are many, and are worth considering as a budget-wise option:

- Rail networks link all areas, urban and rural, as they weave through Europe;
- Train stations are generally situated in the city hub, close to all amenities;
- It's a comfortable way to view the countryside you've travelled so far to see;
- It provides great flexibility for impromptu stopovers;
- It allows you to interact with many interesting local and foreign travellers;
- It saves the cost of accommodations, if you choose overnight travel;
- It saves the cost and risks associated with vehicle rentals;
- Most European trains have wagons dedicated to bicycles;
- Unlike with air travel, there are no security hassles; you need not arrive until just before departure time.

We have often travelled by rail in Europe. As always, we have learned some lessons. A few are worth passing on:

With friends, we backpacked for a month through Europe. Our transportation was by train, using for the first time, our Eurail passes.

the naked traveller

In Italy, intent on joining other Canadian friends in La Spezia in the Cinqueterre area, we rushed to make our train connection.

*We **knew** that in Europe you can almost set your watch, by the precise arrivals and departures of trains.*

Wives trailing behind, Bob and I galloped along the platform. A number of other tourists, headed to the same destination, followed. We made it to the track where our imminent departure time was prominently displayed overhead; passengers were boarding. Bob and I hopped aboard with our little band following, like lemmings!

We settled comfortably into our empty First-Class compartment, congratulating ourselves on having made it just in time.

Sometime later, as she attempted to follow our progress on a route map, Gaye exclaimed that she could not find any of the stations we continued to roll through without stopping. Eventually, we realized that we were heading in the opposite direction, away from our destination!

It finally dawned on us that more than one train departed the station at the same time, from different tracks; we had climbed aboard the wrong one!

"No problem," we announced. We would simply get off at the next station, and reverse our direction. Easier said than done! We were stuck on an Express through-train which was not due to stop for another two hours!

We sheepishly shared our discovery with the other followers, and finally disembarked, to wait another hour and a half (in a local trattoria with a delightful wine menu), for a train going our way.

We eventually did arrive at our destination—almost six hours later than planned! Our long-suffering friends had watched three different trains come and go, before we finally put in an abashed appearance. Dinner was on us that evening!

I think *our* lesson in this was to stop, look, and listen to our wives instead of following our instinct! After that adventure, they refused to follow us onto any further train, without first verifying that it was the correct one.

The lesson for you, the well-informed traveller, would be:

- Verify *details* of train platforms, destinations, departure times, **before** boarding, by carefully reading the highly-visible, easy-to-read electronic display board on each platform, or often simply by asking the conductor or another passenger who is boarding.

- When things do not go according to plan, *go with the flow*. It is not the end of the world. Find something in the situation to enjoy or appreciate. Our little group of "leaders and lemmings" sat, waiting for the right train, in a sunny outdoor café, sampling the local wine and swapping travel misadventure stories.

....

If purchasing a train pass is not part of your plan *before* leaving home, and you later decide to travel by train, check out the local fare rates, rules, and exemptions.

Some countries in Europe will for example, extend a 50% discount to travellers 60 years of age or over. In others, reduced fares are offered between peak commuter-travel times on work days. In many countries, economical daily, weekly, or even monthly passes are available.

Second-Class travel is in most cases, more than adequate, and much less expensive than First Class. The seats *may* be somewhat less plush, but they are generally so comfortable, you may think you stepped into First-Class by accident!

Even with our First-Class Eurail pass, we have often chosen to sit in the more open Second-Class car, sharing picnic meals and halting conversations with the many locals who for economic reasons, tend to favour Second-Class travel. At times, the only travellers we have encountered in First-Class, were other North American tourists with Eurail passes. While it is fun chatting and comparing notes with them, we go to Europe to immerse ourselves in the local culture.

....

Always remember, during your trip-planning stage: the Internet is your best buddy, as an invaluable and quick aide for research into all your travel options.

3. BUS PASSES

The ultimate form of economy travel, other than on foot or bicycle, is by bus. Bus travel will often cost 50% less than by train. Some long-distance bus companies offer city-to-city, hop-on, hop-off bus passes on a predetermined circuit throughout Europe.

Although bus travel has long been a favourite of impoverished students, many travellers today, of all ages and economic means, are choosing to take advantage of this flexible option. Today's bus travel tends to be very comfortable, and thank goodness, smoke-free almost everywhere!

Some buses are super-luxurious, with sleeping berths, food service, video entertainment, and sometimes, bicycle storage.

Bus travel *can* on occasion, be even more efficient than train travel. Bus networks will often cover the more remote areas not served by rail. A point-to-point train journey with stops at every hamlet, can take longer than an Express bus to the same destination.

For starters in your research for Europe's bus pass travel, google *Eurolines Europass*, and *Busabout Pass*. Closer to home, check out *Greyhound Discovery Pass*, serving Canada and the U.S.

TIP # 18 ..... Plane, train and bus passes are a terrific way of achieving great value while maintaining travel flexibility. Research these options carefully to choose the right one for your trip.

CHAPTER EIGHT

COMPENSATION - FLIGHT DELAYS

As anyone who travels often knows very well, sooner or later you will experience a major flight delay, a missed connection, or even be bumped from a reserved flight. Aside from the very real frustration and inconvenience, the savvy traveller is aware of his right in certain circumstances, to compensation from the airline. He knows as well, how to turn a flight delay into a potentially acceptable opportunity.

1. JURISDICTIONAL VARIATIONS

In every country, its air-travel regulator sets out precise rules outlining the minimum compensation which airlines *are required* to offer inconvenienced passengers, in specific situations. These rules of course, do not apply in the case of service suspensions resulting from bankruptcy of an airline.

Before travelling between countries, take advantage of your access to the web. Google, for the appropriate country, *Compensation for Flight Delays and Overbookings*. It is useful to be aware of these requirements, in advance of your trip. They are the specified legal minimums, upon which you may be able to improve, *if* the particular situation should arise.

The European Union has an excellent site at *www.apr.europa.eu* which will give you all the information you are likely to require.

Similarly, *www.airsafe.com/complain/bumping.htm* will assist you in the United States. Canada is still struggling at press time to finalize a comprehensive Bill of Rights for passengers. Until it does, only the protection provided by the *Montreal Convention*, and by the policies of individual airlines, will prevail in Canada.

2. WEATHER DELAYS / ACTS OF GOD

Generally, no compensation will be available in the case of weather-related or other delays which are beyond the control of the airline.

3. AIRLINE - CONTROLLABLE DELAYS

Generally, significant delays within the control of an airline result in its being held accountable for compensating its inconvenienced passengers.

Different rules and degrees of compensation apply in each jurisdiction, their severity dependent on the length of delay. Compensation will generally begin for flight delays exceeding two hours; it may increase for delays greater than four hours; even more so, for overnight delays.

Short delays *may* qualify passengers for meal vouchers and telephone calls only. Longer delays *may* require an airline to provide overnight accommodation, meals, taxis, and telephone calls, as well as cash compensation or flight vouchers.

In the European Community for example, regulations entitle delayed or denied passengers to cash compensation of between 125 and 600 euros, depending on the distance booked, and the length of the delay.

As referred to earlier, pressure for a similar North American "Passenger Bill of Rights" is emerging, and is being debated in both Canada and the United States; it may become reality in the next few years.

4. OVERBOOKED FLIGHTS

Most jurisdictions permit airlines to deliberately overbook their flights. This is in recognition that on most planes there will tend to be a certain number of "no-shows". This practice however, *can* result in major inconvenience to those passengers who are left behind at the boarding gate. The mandated compensation in this eventuality, tends to be at its most generous, for these displaced passengers.

In an attempt to avoid ill-will among passengers, many airlines call for volunteers willing to delay their travel, in return for generous incentives—often far more attractive than those mandated by regulation.

For example, it is not uncommon for airlines to offer hundreds of dollars in cash compensation, in addition to meal vouchers and telephone calls; when necessary, good quality hotel accommodation is included. If the first call for volunteers leaves the flight with still too many passengers, the agent will often increase the reward, enticing takers until enough seats are freed up.

As an added incentive to free up overbooked seats, some airlines will offer a travel voucher, redeemable for a future flight to any of their destinations. This is *in addition* to getting you to your original destination, on the next available flight.

Whenever we have seen such offers being made, a number of passengers have rushed the desk, already planning their free trip, as they offer to give up their seats. When too many volunteers have come forward, the airline agent accepts offers in the order in which they are received.

*Our sister and brother-in-law frequently fly back and forth between Los Angeles and Vancouver, a particularly busy and often overbooked route. Both retired, they have a flexible schedule. Knowing that these flights are often overbooked, they have acquired the habit of **always offering** upon check-in, to be bumped if necessary. That way, they are usually among the first passengers offered free ticket-*

vouchers if the plane is overbooked. On at least a third of their trips they are offered a delay. They happily take the next available flight, and accept vouchers for a pair of free tickets. For the sake of a few hours' delay, they have free round-trip tickets for their next trip, some months later!

Airlines naturally prefer to have passengers advise them in advance, of a willingness to accept a delay. This allows them to solve an over-booking problem without having to announce it on the P.A. system. They simply call the willing passengers by name, to report to the counter.

TIP # 19 ..... When travelling by air, know in advance, your rights and the airline's obligations, should you be bumped off a flight, or offered a delay incentive.

While travelling on business with an airline on which I was a frequent passenger, I arrived in plenty of time to board a commuter plane, small enough that it had no assigned seats. Not knowing it was overbooked, I took my time boarding, only to find that every seat was occupied! No announcement had been made about the plane being overbooked, nor had there been a call for volunteers. This was the last flight out that day. As a result, I was forced to stay overnight in the small community, far from my next day's early-morning meeting with major customers. Needless to say, I was not impressed!

When I finally arrived at my office the next day, I asked my assistant to call the airline's customer service department, to advise them of the circumstances, and to ask what they proposed to do about it.

As well as receiving a letter of apology from a senior official at the airline, I was offered a free excursion for my entire family to our choice of any of its Canadian destinations. Some months later, we enjoyed an all-expense paid, three-day and two-night, fully-guided fishing trip on the Skeena River, in Terrace, BC.

Yes, I was at the time, a "Super Elite" client of that airline. All airlines however, usually want to keep *all* their customers happy, regardless of how often they fly. Airlines will generally do everything reasonable, to avoid alienation of loyalties.

My 85-year old mother flew in December, across Canada to visit us in Victoria. On the return flight to London, Ontario, her connecting flight, from Calgary to London, was suddenly cancelled. She and her fellow passengers were put on a flight an hour later, to Hamilton, Ontario. After arriving there, exhausted and quite upset, she and two others were put into a taxi, at 1:00 a.m., for the long road trip to London, in the middle of winter! She arrived at her dark, silent Senior's residence at 3:00 a.m., about five hours later than originally scheduled.

I very quickly called the airline to politely express my displeasure. They immediately offered my mother a travel voucher, to be redeemed within the next year.

The airline was very responsive, once I challenged their actions. Had I not done so however, no compensation would have been offered.

TIP # 20 .... If you, or a family member, experience a major inconvenience within an airline's control, and if you are not offered immediate, acceptable compensation, follow-up your concerns. Make a phone call. If necessary, send a letter to a senior executive at the airline. Often, an e-mail will suffice and will usually result in a prompt and reasonable reply.

Our daughter received an airline voucher with no expiry date on it. When she tried to use it 13 months later, she was told that it had expired. No shrinking violet, she challenged the airline, and after several e-mails and phone calls, received not only an apology but also a new voucher and extra points for her mileage plan. The airline also informed her that they were immediately clarifying their policy to avoid future misunderstandings.

The airline business is very competitive world-wide. Most airlines recognize that one unhappy customer can quickly spread the word of a negative experience to many others. Airlines would rather that a passenger spread the word about the fair treatment or compensation he received after an unfortunate event occurred.

CHAPTER NINE

BAGGAGE HASSLES

1. WEIGHT LIMITS

The price of fuel has skyrocketed over the past few years. Airlines have not only imposed regular fuel surcharges, but also, have drastically cut baggage-weight allowances. If they could do so in a politically-correct manner, they would doubtless weigh each passenger as well as his luggage!

The most frustrating part of these changes is a lack of consistency throughout the industry. Not all airlines have set the same limits and allowances. If you find yourself connecting from one carrier to another, you can get caught between two differing weight limits, with the result that you may have to pay a significant excess-weight penalty.

Several years ago when we flew to Mexico for a six-week winter getaway, the generous per-person baggage allowance was two checked bags, at 70 pounds apiece. On the return flight with exactly the same luggage weight, and the same carrier, we were shocked to learn that the allowance had, in the interim, dropped to 50 pounds per bag! No matter how hard we tried to get around it, we ended up having to pay $100 per bag, in excess-weight penalties!

One way to be prepared, particularly if checking only one bag, is to pack an empty, soft-sided bag, such as a gym bag. If you then encounter an unexpected weight issue, you can simply split the contents into the second bag, and check it as well, thereby avoiding costly penalties.

Be aware though, that in 2008, some airlines began charging for *each* bag checked, regardless of weight, even if below the allowable limit! Some airlines also apply a total-checked-baggage weight restriction per passenger, regardless of the number of bags.

We have found European carriers to be both strict, and expensive. This seems especially so with the discount carriers. Your basic ticket may be a bargain, but the more luggage you have, the more your costs escalate, and quite dramatically so. We have listened to passengers in check-in lines in Europe, grumbling that their baggage charges far exceeded the cost of their ticket!

In 2008 our daughter and her family flew home from Europe on a discount carrier. The checked-baggage allowance was one bag for each of three passengers, not to exceed 20 kg each. Aware of these restrictions, they packed very carefully, leaving behind worn shoes, toiletries, and even unread novels. When weighed at the check-in counter, each of their three bags was two kg over the allowance. The excess-baggage charge amounted to 15 euros per kilo, for a total of 90 euros, or about $150!

In past years, such a minor excess-weight would have raised hardly an eyebrow at check-in, let alone attracted an extra charge.

The small print on your ticket will detail your baggage allowances. However, they can often be confusing. Does "20 kg total" mean 20 kg per bag, or is it the combined weight allowance for both bags? Phone the airline's 1-800 number and check any ambiguities, before leaving for the airport.

Never assume that the luggage rules which applied on your last trip, or even at the outset of your current travels, have remained unchanged.

....

Carry-on baggage has not escaped the air carriers' attention either.

Some of us will remember the days of boarding a return flight from Hawaii, only to find our carry-on bag sharing the cramped overhead storage compartment with the paraphernalia of other vacationers who had struggled on board with everything except a palm tree. Well, no longer!

Hand-carry luggage weight-and-size limits again vary greatly, from airline to airline. We have been subjected to allowances as low as 5 kg, and as high as 15 kg. Carriers everywhere, particularly in Europe, are becoming more and more adamant about enforcing their rules. We have been caught out a number of times, forced at check-in to shuffle items between our hand-carry bags, in order to balance the weight of each.

TIP # 21 ..... **Check the baggage rules very carefully for each airline on which you fly during a trip; make sure that your bag sizes and weights conform, if there are differences, to the limits of the carrier with the most stringent requirements.**

---

2. LOST LUGGAGE

One of the most frustrating events associated with air travel is the inevitable experience of lost or delayed luggage . Most of us have, or will, experience this at least once, if we travel enough.

Despite technological advances, lost or mishandled luggage is a growing problem for travellers. U.S. government statistics indicate that incidents involving lost, delayed, damaged, or pilfered luggage, increased by 16% between 2005 and 2007.

You can take steps to *somewhat* reduce this risk, and if a misrouting occurs, to shorten the time it takes for the airline to reunite you and your luggage:

- Always update your name tag on *each* piece of luggage, be it checked or carry-on, with your current destination. On an extended trip involving several stopovers, carry and attach a new label for each stopover.

- Do not attach the destination tag to the main handle that baggage handlers automatically grab when transferring your bags.

- Inside every checked bag, on top of the contents, leave a copy of your entire trip itinerary, with forwarding addresses, even if only hotel names, for each segment of your trip.

- In order to fully describe a lost bag to airline authorities, consider carrying a photograph of your bags, along with other important documents, in your hand-carry luggage. Some experienced travellers even carry an inventory list of the contents of their checked luggage, to facilitate potential insurance claims.

- Consider exchanging, or otherwise uniquely identifying, your basic black suitcase, similar to hundreds of others on each flight, for luggage that stands out from the rest. Put your creativity to the test.

The above are common-sense preventative steps to take. They do you little good however, if your luggage has failed to arrive in Miami, and you are due to leave within a few hours on a Caribbean Cruise!

What to do in that case? No, don't scream and yell and harass the agent!

- Have your itinerary, baggage-check receipts, and I.D. at the ready.

- When reporting the missing bags to the airline's agent at the airport, confirm the details of their compensation policies for the immediate purchase of emergency-replacement items.

- Be familiar with the compensation policies and limits of your credit card. Gold and platinum cards in particular, will be the most generous. *Always* keep your boarding passes and luggage checks. These must usually accompany any claims.

- When purchasing your travel medical protection, consider purchasing an *all-encompassing policy* which, aside from health and trip cancellation protection, usually provides generous lost-luggage compensation.

- Review your Homeowner's insurance policy. Albeit possibly with a hefty deductible, it may provide coverage in the event of a permanent loss.

All of your efforts may help to mitigate the economic cost of lost or delayed luggage. They do not however, eliminate the huge inconvenience you still face.

Be warned; the claims procedure for all of these financial recoveries can be a real time-consuming nuisance! But persevere; you will, some weeks later, receive at least partial restitution.

The worst scenario is that your bag is permanently lost or stolen, never to be seen again! The Montreal Convention, to which most North American and European countries subscribe, considers a bag to be *lost* if it remains missing more than 21 days. It also sets the airline's liability cap at around U.S. $1,600 per suitcase.

A senior member of our family experienced the nerve-wracking ordeal of losing a bag packed with family albums. The major airline involved was not terribly concerned or responsive, until a major newspaper picked up the human interest story. A $1,500 cheque magically arrived within days!

Although this could not replace the lost treasures, the airline did provide restitution of a sort.

Quite reasonably, in the case of a total-loss claim, the airline will expect you to fill out a *detailed* claims form, listing the contents and their estimated value. Not the easiest thing to do in detail, at the best of times.

The fine print accompanying your ticket will try to limit the carrier's liability. Don't expect to make money on this type of loss!

peter dolezal

TIP # 22 ..... Be aware of the financial recovery options available to you, in the event of a delay or loss of
your checked luggage; take every step feasible
to reduce the risk.

....

In fairness, in the greatest majority of cases, an airline courier, your misrouted luggage in hand, will catch up to you, often the same day, or within a few days.

Recognize that with air travel, the risk is there. Be prepared. Carry an emergency clothing change, important documents, medications and priceless items like family albums, in your hand-carry luggage. With the ever stricter weight-limits on cabin luggage, even this precaution is becoming more challenging.

Having travelled a great deal, both on business and for pleasure, we have found that the only sure way to eliminate the risk of lost or delayed luggage, is to travel ultra-light, with only carry-on cabin luggage. This has proven to be practical for most short trips, but nigh impossible for a six-week winter holiday!

Many knowledgeable business travellers absolutely refuse to check luggage, due to the risk of loss or delayed delivery.

TIP # 23..... If at all feasible, avoid all checked-baggage and
lost-luggage issues by travelling only with the
maximum permissible carry-on baggage, and no
checked-baggage.

CHAPTER TEN

SECURITY ISSUES

1. AIRLINE SECURITY

In the not-too-distant past, travel security was a quick and fairly routine exercise, rarely delaying flights and passengers. Today, every traveller must be tuned in to the ever-evolving levels of security-consciousness at airports, whether domestic or international, and their ramifications for all air travellers.

Be aware of a few basic procedures. Adhering to them will ensure that your air travel experience is as hassle-free as possible:

- Arrive well in advance of flight times, particularly for international flights.
- Follow strictly, the current restrictions on allowable contents of cabin-luggage.
- Don't lock your checked bags, to facilitate security checks.
- Wear easily-removed footwear for security checks.
- Don't send your cabin items through the screening apparatus until just before you yourself step through the personal screening system.
- Keep your eye glued to your laptop, wallet and other valuables as they pass through security screening.
- Do not joke about ANY aspect of security, at any airport.
- Make sure your checked baggage is very distinctively marked, so that you can quickly and easily spot your bags as soon as they appear on the baggage carousel.

- Above all, remain patient, calm and flexible. The system will not change just because you become agitated!

These approaches seem rather self-evident. However, I am always amazed at how many travellers, including ourselves in the past, were either not aware, or simply ignored these protocols.

Some years ago, we had as always, locked our checked bags. When we collected them at our destination, the lock on one of the bags had been rather brutally mangled. Clearly, security personnel had chosen to inspect the bag. We were later told that a system of random security checks on that flight had flagged our bag for a manual search. That explained the big "X" we found chalked on the bag. We have not locked our bags since!

Today, such checks are no longer random. Most airports now subject *every* piece of checked baggage to electronic screening. Any unusual image will result in an automatic manual examination. As a result of this more exacting process, you are much more likely to have your bags searched. Any lock on the bag will simply be cut off or forced open. **Don't lock your checked bags!** At most, to keep zippers closed, use a twist-tie.

On more than one occasion we have encountered dismayed air-travellers whose laptop or wallet had disappeared - right in front of them! As they waited their turn to walk through the security sensor, their carry-on possessions proceeded well ahead of them, on the conveyor through the x-ray machine. By the time they caught up with their belongings, one or more items had gone missing!

It helps to throw your jacket, which you must take off, over your smaller, more valuable items. You may even prefer to slip your wallet and other valuables into your jacket pocket, before placing it in the plastic bin. This should make them less visible and accessible to sticky fingers.

We once encountered in our hotel tired travellers who, on arriving at the hotel, discovered that they had picked up a stranger's bag. Their own bags were identical, and had no distinct markings. The couple had not checked the name tags or baggage checks at the carousel.

Imagine the hassle ! One exhausted traveller with the wrong bag; another distraught traveller with no bag; and an unmarked, unclaimed bag at the airport's "Lost Luggage" desk—all the elements of a bad movie! And so easily avoidable!

To ensure that we travel with *somewhat* distinctive bags, we have for many years secured around each bag, a brightly-coloured, but easily removable belt. This is not foolproof however; several times the belt has gone missing between check-in and retrieval. Lately we have added brightly-coloured fabric tape around each handle.

TIP # 24 ..... Accept the new security realities as a fact of life; tune in to them, and take simple steps to minimize their impact on your travel.

---

2. PERSONAL SECURITY

Some travellers limit their foreign travel simply because they hear of, and react to, occasional incidents and tragedies which are reported, extensively, in their local or national media.

This concern is for the most part, unwarranted.

One winter, when the European media reported, at length, that Canada was screening its air passengers for a particularly nasty, but very rare virus, we received panicked phone calls from Europe, begging us to cancel our planned visit. Our trip was still eight months in the future! Given the manner in which their media had treated the story, local concerns were understandable, but the danger was grossly exaggerated. The panic worsened as our departure date

*approached. We eventually cancelled our trip, with a totally unnec-
essary loss of tourist income for that community and for the country.*

At home we don't stop driving because road accidents have occurred,
even when injuries or worse, death, have resulted. But we do take precautions. We strive to drive a mechanically-sound car, we drive defen-
sively, and we adjust our driving to suit the conditions. This does not
eliminate our risk when driving; but it does reduce that risk to what
we consider, prudent levels.

This is exactly the same approach to use in travelling. If we are careless in
the way we flash our cash, or carry purses, wallets, and other valuables,
we are at some risk of being victimized, even in our own home town.

Being extra cautious, when travelling in different cultures and economic environments, is only prudent; but one should not become par-
anoid! A few commonsense practices will greatly reduce the personal
risks of international travel:

- Leave your fancy watch and jewelry at home, or in your safety
  deposit box. Limit yourself to an inexpensive watch and cos-
  tume jewelry.

  *We prefer water-resistant watches with a fabric band. We
  find them to be more comfortable in humid environments,
  and we don't have to remove them to go for a swim. More-
  over, they certainly do not look worth stealing!*

- If you have an obviously expensive engagement ring, wear
  your plainer wedding band, but consider leaving the one with
  the rock at home.

- If you are an unmarried woman, whether travelling solo or in a
  group, consider wearing a plain wedding band simply to ward
  off unwelcome attention.

- Try to avoid carrying prominent handbags, wallets, or cameras that attract attention. If you carry a fanny pack, adopt the
  kangaroo look and wear your pouch at the front. Keep a hand
  on all bags at all times, especially in crowds.

- Dress as close to the look of a starving student as you feel comfortable. Travel-oriented clothing such as Canada's Tilley line, for instance, is particularly suitable for its easy-pack, understated elegance, along with its velcroed and *secret* pockets.

   Keep in mind however, that as we travellers become more clever in our precautions, so do those who inspire the precautions. Street urchins the world over, are quick to learn many of our tricks and hiding places.

- Especially when travelling in less-developed countries, use cash. Minimize the use of your credit card to pay for purchases. Never let your card out of your sight.

If paying with your card at a restaurant, insist that the waiter bring the imprint machine to your table. If this is impossible, either go with him to the terminal, or pull out your cash.

Friends who used their credit card in a restaurant in Mexico failed to keep sight of their card. To their dismay, two days later, they found that the card was not useable. When they phoned the credit card company, they were advised that a "hold" had been placed on their card due to several thousand dollars of unusual purchases the previous day. Someone, presumably at the restaurant, had made a duplicate imprint. From it, a duplicate card had been produced and used fraudulently, all within 24 hours!

While your credit card company will keep you whole in such fraudulent use instances, the inconvenience of obtaining a replacement card outside North America, can be considerable.

Credit cards which require you to enter a pin number in lieu of a signature, reduce the above risk *somewhat,* as long as your card does not encounter a rigged machine which retains your pin number!

Except in an absolute emergency, or when making a major transportation purchase, we never use a credit card when travelling outside North America.

We prefer instead to use a debit card at a local ATM, and try to pay cash for virtually everything. Yes, we are giving up the chance to increase our reward-miles account, but when travelling, we choose prudence over points.

- Withdrawing cash from an ATM? Try, if at all possible, to avoid using an on-street site. If it's your only option, have someone with you, and make your withdrawal in daylight hours. Remember too, to retrieve your receipt *and* your card - quickly!

We once spent half a day on a Monday, at a small bank in Mexico. Our bank card had been gobbled up by the cash machine on the week-end. I had not removed the card quickly enough, and the machine was programmed to "eat" any card not withdrawn within 15 seconds. We were one of six couples in the bank that morning, all there for the same reason!

These simple precautions will greatly reduce your chance of attracting fraud artists or pickpockets, your greatest on-street risks when travelling.

....

Before leaving home, do your homework. Educate yourself on your destination: not only its attractions, but also its risks. Libraries, book stores, and the web, all offer a multitude of travel insights for every conceivable destination.

Although we always refer to a wide range of resources, we have become aficionados of the Rick Steves series for our European travels, and the Lonely Planet series for other destinations. Using these and other guides alerts us to extraordinary precautions it would be wise to heed, in specific locations.

As an added precaution, we have always carried in our hand-luggage, a photocopy of all important documents, such as passports, driver's licenses, tickets, travel insurance documents, medical information and credit cards, just in case any originals are lost or stolen.

Replacement arrangements are much easier if you have copies at hand. An even more efficient method, is to scan all necessary documents into your computer, then transfer all the data onto a key-sized flash drive. This is much easier and lighter to carry than a stack of paper.

Several of our friends have lost cameras to thieves. In reporting the theft to local police, the first question they were always asked was, "What is the make and serial number?". The manufacturer they knew, but not the serial number. We now have a record of serial numbers for all electronic items we carry. We leave one set at home, and carry the other on the flash drive.

Some travellers who lose a replaceable item such as a camera, don't even bother to report the loss to local police, knowing that the process will be time-consuming and very unlikely to result in an early recovery of the item.

The loss of your passport, on the other hand, creates chaos and hardship. Without your passport you are helpless. It may take you days to reach the nearest embassy and to obtain a temporary replacement passport. Be extra vigilant in safeguarding it.

If the missing item is sufficiently valuable to claim the loss on your homeowner's policy, be forewarned. Your insurance company will always expect you to submit a copy of a *police report* with your claim. In the absence of such a report, your claim may well be rejected.

TIP # 25 ..... Before travelling, educate yourself on the pros and cons of your destination. Take common-sense measures to minimize the risk of becoming a target of petty crime - pickpockets in particular.

....

At any given time, certain destinations should clearly be avoided. If political or civil unrest exists in a region, it makes sense to delay your visit until the situation has settled down. Both the U.S. and Canadian governments routinely issue travel and health *advisories*. Pay attention to them, and take them seriously. Be aware too, that by travelling *against* official advice, you may in fact invalidate some, or even all, of your travel and health insurance.

Most travel destinations appear, on the surface, to be relatively stable. But within the borders of many, including many regions of Africa, Asia, Central and South America, are huge pockets of extreme poverty, with high crime rates. Again, detailed travel books, the media, and *current* government advisories, will educate and guide you, in the appropriate precautions for your travels.

Several years ago, we travelled with friends for a month, throughout South Africa. For the first time, we chose to take a comprehensive organized tour, rather than our usual independent travel approach. We did not regret this decision. It was a memorable, incident-free trip, much of it in a very comfortable bus, with excellent guides, accommodation, and a varied and eye-opening itinerary. We were privileged to experience an extremely emotional, but educational visit to one of the larger Townships outside Capetown. An independent traveller, on the other hand, would have been advised at that time, to avoid the Townships.

Had we elected to travel independently, as was the norm for both our friends and ourselves, I'm sure we would have as always, enjoyed our trip. This was one time however, when we were pleased to leave the arrangements and security measures to a recommended local tour organizer, whose very livelihood depended on keeping his clients healthy and safe. Our decision certainly eliminated a lot of stress that we might otherwise have experienced.

3. HOME SECURITY

Your home and its contents are precious to you. Simple precautions before travelling, ensure that you return to find your home in the same condition as when you left; or in the event of an unwelcome mishap, that you are adequately protected from any loss.

- Re-read your home insurance policy. Some policies require that your empty house be checked every three or four days, to avoid issues arising in some claims, such as for water damage. Make the necessary arrangements to ensure compliance with your policy.

- Stop newspaper delivery at least a day before you leave, to personally confirm that it has been stopped. Nothing advertises your absence more visibly, than a stack of yellowed papers on your doorstep.

- Arrange for lawn and garden care, to minimize external evidence of your absence.

- Consider taking advantage of a reasonably-priced service offered by the Post Office. At your request, they will hold all of your mail for the period of your absence; the accumulated bundle will be delivered to you, on your specified restart date.

- If you travel frequently or for extended periods, consider having a remotely-monitored security system. Before going away, call the security firm to inform them of your planned absence. Advise them of any individuals whom you have authorized to visit or stay in your home while you are absent.

- Be both safety-conscious and frugal. Turn down hot water tanks and heating systems. Turn off lamps, computers, and other electronics. Unplug small appliances.

- Should your plans include having someone stay in your home during your absence, again be prepared. Tell them when the mail will arrive, when to put out the garbage, and what message to give telephone callers. Telling strangers that the owners are on vacation can be an open invitation to a problem.

Most of these suggestions are little more than basic common sense. But incorporating them into your planning will help ensure that you remember your holiday for its memorable experiences, and not for the shock of a nasty surprise on the day you return home.

CHAPTER ELEVEN

TRAVEL INSURANCE

1. HEALTH INSURANCE

If your travels involve leaving the country, even for a short day-trip between Canada and the U.S., **do NOT cross an international border without first purchasing medical insurance coverage.**

Even when we accompany our grandchildren on a brief day-trip for a soccer game across the border in the U.S., we always arrange medical coverage for everyone.

For foreign travellers requiring medical assistance while visiting the U.S. in particular, the financial consequences of travelling without insurance can be absolutely devastating. Not only foolhardy, this risk is preventable, usually at a very reasonable cost.

Who doesn't know of someone who has visited a doctor or an emergency department in a U.S. hospital, only to be faced with huge costs, at times amounting to several thousand dollars?

One of our friends suffers from severe food allergies which have landed him in numerous emergency departments world-wide, including in the U.S. Fortunate to have had life-saving access to their services, he has saved many tens of thousands of dollars over the years, by purchasing before his travels, the appropriate health insurance.

We have all heard or read of visitors to the U.S. who have had to undergo an emergency heart angioplasty, or even open-heart surgery, wherein the final bill was in the several hundred thousands of dollars!

This astronomical cost is the reason why, rather than have you undergo surgery in the U.S., travel health insurers will usually arrange your evacuation back to your own country, even if they have to charter a jet. Even a $20,000 emergency air evacuation, with a medical attendant accompanying you, is a bargain for the insurer when compared to the alternative.

Before our recent Amazon travels, we were required to provide written evidence of a health insurance plan which included emergency evacuation coverage from remote locations.

Many options exist for the purchase of such insurance, even on-line. Many credit card companies sell it, as do financial institutions, automobile associations and, of course, travel agencies and insurance companies. The cost is related to your age and health history. Given the protection and peace of mind it provides, it is extremely inexpensive, worthwhile, and a great value.

If, due to a major health issue, you happen to be uninsurable for travel, **do not travel outside your own country,** where your health coverage is assured. Both Canada and the U.S. are such large and fascinating countries, that even if you are restricted to travel adventures within your own borders, you can enjoy years of interesting, varied holidays.

*When planning our next adventure, we **always** factor in the cost of travel health insurance, as an integral part of our travel budget.*

2. TRIP CANCELLATION, INTERRUPTION, AND BAGGAGE INSURANCE

This type of insurance is truly discretionary for the wise traveller. Unlike health insurance protection which one should *always* accept as a necessary part of the travel budget, the need to cancel or interrupt your trip due to for instance, an unforeseen family emergency, or the loss of your luggage, while very upsetting, are generally not issues that could result in wiping you out financially.

Most insurance plans will offer either medical coverage alone, or will package it into a **comprehensive plan**, together with cancellation, interruption, and baggage protection. In most cases, the decision whether to buy solely the medical protection, versus the comprehensive plan, will come down to questions of *peace of mind*. For the modest extra cost, many travellers will opt for the full coverage.

If you travel often, as we do, or if you enjoy taking advantage of last-minute travel bargains, consider membership in an **annual plan.** Under this umbrella coverage, you are protected for as many trips as you may wish to take during the coverage year, up to a specified number of days (often 35) for each trip taken. The coverage typically provides a comprehensive plan that varies in cost with one's age and medical history.

My wife and I belong to such a plan. We pay, for the two of us, about $50 per month for unlimited, protected travel anywhere in the world. We are not required to notify the insurance company of planned travel, as long as we do not exceed the specified 35-days-per-trip. If we plan a longer absence, we simply notify the insurer, well in advance, and pay a surcharge for the extra days' coverage.

Numerous insurance plans are available; some by payroll deduction, others through pension plans. Most North American Automobile Association organizations offer such plans, along with individual trip coverage. Simply google *Travel Insurance* to find the many sources, and specific coverage options.

When buying travel insurance *packages*, the most costly elements are the medical, trip cancellation, and trip interruption coverage. The price will vary substantially, depending most particularly on your age, health history, and trip duration. Shop around between various providers for best-value coverage for your needs. Read the fine print, to ensure that you really have chosen the best.

TIP # 26 ..... NEVER risk financial catastrophe by travelling internationally without Travel Health Insurance coverage. For extra peace of mind, consider the discretionary addition of supplemental coverage for trip cancellation, trip interruption, and baggage insurance.

---

3. FARE - PAYMENT INSURANCE

Always try to pay your airline, tour operator or travel agent with a **credit card**, rather than by debit card, cash or cheque. This usually provides you with automatic protection of the amount you have prepaid, should any of these travel providers become insolvent or bankrupt, before you have completed your trip.

Most credit cards will refund your payment, if you can demonstrate that the service which you purchased with their card, was not delivered through no fault of your own. Check your credit card agreement for details of payment rules, which must be followed to qualify for this protection.

In recent years a number of North American tour operators, most notably charter airlines, have either temporarily suspended operations, sought creditor protection, or declared bankruptcy. As a result, some have defaulted on their obligations to customers, unable to repay fares already received. Clients who had paid with credit cards were the more fortunate. Generally, they were able to receive full restitution. Without that protection, many others lost most, or even all, of their prepayment.

In 2008 we purchased round-trip tickets from Vancouver, BC to Paris, France. Three weeks before we were due to return, our carrier, Zoom Airlines, moved into creditor protection status and ceased operations with no notice. It required much effort to find *new tickets at a reasonable price, for our return flight. Most sched-uled airlines wanted $3,000 to $4,000 per ticket, for the one-way trip. Finally, through the internet, we learned that Air Berlin had seats on a direct flight from Dusseldorf, Germany to Vancouver, at a cost of only $750 per person. This was roughly what we had paid on Zoom. While we incurred some inconvenience and cost in hav-ing to get to Dusseldorf, we made it home on schedule. Once home, a simple phone call to our credit card company, followed by a fax copy of our Zoom Electronic Ticket, and a month later, we received a full credit on our account for the amount we had paid for the un-used portion of our return ticket with Zoom.*

Had we not used a credit card to pay for our Zoom tickets, we would have been out of pocket not only the considerable extra costs of re-turning home with another carrier, but also the full amount we had paid Zoom.

4. LIFE AND DISABILITY INSURANCE

Many credit cards offer travellers at *no extra cost*, life and disability insurance. Usually, this is applicable in the event of disability or death arising from travel on public transport, while on a trip which was pur-chased on that card.

This insurance limit can be as high as $500,000. Not something you would ever wish to collect on, but well-worth having, since it is free extra coverage.

Read the fine print. Should *your* card provide this coverage, ensure that your family or next-of-kin are aware of it. If, in the event of a trag-edy, someone fails to apply for this benefit within the specified time frame, the benefit could be lost.

Of course, eligibility for this coverage is predicated on your charging your travel cost to your credit card.

TIP # 27 ..... Always try to book your trip using your favourite, rewards-earning credit card, in order to secure the probable right to a refund of your payment, in the event of non-performance; and possibly, to provide you with extra life and disability coverage. Check specific provisions with your card issuer.

IT BEARS REPEATING.....

Pay off that credit card balance as soon as you can, to minimize interest charges.

· ·

CHAPTER TWELVE

ACCOMMODATION

Have you dreamed of one day staying in a tree-top safari lodge? A yurt? An ice hotel? Or are you content with a simple room with just a pillow and blanket?

One of the most expensive elements of travel tends to be the cost of accommodation. It is worthwhile therefore, to investigate the varied options for obtaining the best-possible value, on any budget.

1. HOSTELS

Hostels are for the younger, the elder, or the adventurous and frugal traveller of any age. Hostels abound in most countries worldwide. A bonus, they are generally located in the city core, with easy access to all forms of public transit. Check out *www.hihostels.com*.

Aside from their significant price advantage, the attraction of hostelling is the *communal living*, an opportunity to meet and interact with a microcosm of the world, under one roof.

This mode of inexpensive, rent-a-bed lodging enjoys a wide following among travellers of all ages and economic means. For the solo traveller in particular, it provides an opportunity to mingle and connect, in a safe and friendly environment. Generally more flexible in their travel plans, hostellers delight in adjusting their itineraries as they forge new international friendships.

The term "*hostel*" often conjures up images of a noisy, glorified bunkhouse, with each occupant hauling his own bedroll to avoid picking up unwanted "pets", and down the hall, a single shared bathroom. In some locales this is still the norm.

Amenities vary widely, from hostel to hostel. Most establishments now ban personal bedding, determined to prevent the import of bed-bugs and other pests. While some hostels offer only the basic *dorm*, others have become very attractive destinations in their own right. Some offer private rooms and even private baths, for a modest extra fee. It is not unusual for such accommodation to cost less than half that of a two-star hotel, particularly in Europe. Hostels are indeed so popular, that many impose a limit on the length of one's stay.

In 2008 our young nephew graduated from university. To celebrate his success, he set off on a six-month solo travel adventure, with ex-tremely limited funds. His key objective—to journey as far as pos-sible, as inexpensively as possible. We met up with him in Prague at the end of his fourth month of travel. By that time he had flown from Calgary, Alberta to explore Thailand, Cambodia, Singapore, Vietnam, and the Philippines. He eventually continued on to Lon-don, England, to couch-surf at his sister's, then travelled with her to Austria, Poland, Germany, and the Czech Republic. Other than discount air travel, the cornerstone of his money-stretching effort was hostelling—at times for as little as $3 per night! After 120 days of travel he had spent a total of only $4,900; approximately $40 per day, including all transportation costs! In inflation-adjusted terms, that certainly matches the $10-per-day travel stories of the 1960's.

If *your* objective is to travel widely, at least-possible cost, do not ignore the hostel option, with its networking opportunities and its United Na-tions atmosphere.

2. GUEST HOUSES

As you leave cities behind, to travel the world's highways and lesser roads, you will encounter many privately-run guest-houses. Roughly equivalent to the North American Bed and Breakfast Inn, they differ only in the number of rooms, amenities offered, and price. This type of home-away-from-home accommodation represents excellent value, although in some instances, offerings in castles, monasteries and grand chateaux can rival the prices and luxury of four and five-star hotels.

In continental Europe, guest houses abound, among others, as *Chambre d'Hote, Zimmer Frei, Posada*, and *Pension*. Many of the smaller family-owned-and-operated establishments may have a minimal advertising budget; you will not necessarily find them on a website. These establishments are suited more to on-the-spot bookings, whereby you first inspect the quarters, then decide either to stay, or move on to look at other options. Anxious to supplement their income, the owners are eager to welcome you as their guest. For you, it's an ideal opportunity to experience local hospitality and culture, at the grass-roots level. Longer stays may often result in a reduced rate—and a new friendship.

Equally so, the typical *Bed-and-Breakfast* in rural and small-town North America provides a more personal touch than is usually found in motels or hotels. It fills a very welcome need where there may be little, to no, other available accommodation in the area. B&B's have become so popular however, that an ever-increasing number no longer target the budget-conscious traveller.

In many popular destination cities, resort areas and heritage locales, B&B's have gone upscale, vying with one another to attract the discriminating traveller who is willing to pay a price which often exceeds that of an average family hotel. Each B&B offers a unique experience or setting. Again, as with many European guest houses, some B&B's are in fact, luxurious small inns, in exotic settings, in which the service is impeccable, the amenities awe-inspiring, and the prices astronomical. Generally, these establishments tend to cater to adult travellers; children, while not always turned away, are not welcomed with open arms.

One B&B in our local area has established its niche by catering to pets and their owners, with special dog beds, dog treats, dog videos, and even "dog-sitting" services.

3. MOTELS AND HOTELS

Here the traveller is faced with a myriad of choices. They range from the low-end, small, basic "Ma & Pa" motel, to the budget-motel chains where, outside metropolitan areas, $50 to $60 can still get you a plain, but clean room with kitchenette and private bath.

At the other end of the scale are the $500 per night, high-end Sheratons, Fairmonts, Intercontinentals, Hiltons and the like, with their valet parking, spas, pools, fitness, and business centres. Some travellers, who have the means, prefer the security of the familiar, preferring to stay with these high-end chains where the standards and services present no surprises or challenges.

With little effort, you'll encounter between these two extremes, every possible price, quality and amenities option. Where on this diverse scale you choose to stay, will depend not only on your budget, but also on your specific requirements.

My family well recalls the weekend we set off on a cycling trip to Mayne Island, one of Canada's west coast Gulf Islands. I had managed to book the last available room in the Island's only hotel, for only $20. We rode the ferry, struggled up one mountainous hill after another, visited the local lighthouse, and finally checked into our charming seaside hotel. When we opened the door to our room, it was to the sight of two single beds crowding the room. No one said a word. We simply drew straws—three on the beds, three on the floor. The only place for our shoes was on the ledge outside our window!

Lesson well-learned; for $20 don't expect the Hilton. Our children, now adults, always confirm the amenities before booking accommodation.

4. HOLIDAY RESORTS

Where do more and more multi-generational, extended families congregate to celebrate a special event? At all-in-one, all-inclusive resorts.

Resort accommodations vary greatly, from massive timber lodges, to chalets, cabins and hotel-style suites, to open-sided cabanas on a tropical beach. Vacation accommodations can be found in major natural-wonder beachfront, to mountainside destinations, or in theme and activity-oriented resorts.

Although few of these will be for the true bargain-basement value hunter, they *can* be surprisingly affordable for many families, if a kitchenette or an all-inclusive meal plan is part of the package.

Resort offerings will often be packaged in three-night to multi-week holidays. They are frequently marketed by tour companies or airlines, offering complete vacation packages inclusive of airfare, transfers, meals, on-site activities, and on occasion, extras such as free beverages. Since prices are aimed at the *average*, budget-conscious traveller, they tend to represent great value.

Consider how often we hear of an entire bridal party and its guests, travelling to an exotic setting such as Hawaii, the Caribbean, or Mexico, for a wedding celebration.

Visitors from Europe and Japan have often told us that, even with air fares included, a wedding, or other large celebration, is often much cheaper in Hawaii or Mexico, than had it been celebrated at home!

> **TIP # 28 .....** Accommodations world-wide, offer a huge range of options, to suit all travellers' every price and quality expectation. Regardless of the option selected, realize that price flexibility or inclusions such as free parking or internet access, may exist, often merely by asking!

5. PRIVATE APARTMENTS

It is possible to obtain great value in booking self-contained apartment accommodation in most countries, even for short periods of time. A very useful website is ***www.VRBO.com***, *Vacation Rentals by Owner.* It will guide you in selecting on any continent, and in most countries, a multitude of private apartment options.

6. BOOKING BEST-VALUE

Regardless of whether you are a low-budget traveller, or one who craves luxury all the way, be proactive about achieving best possible value for your holiday dollar.

It is difficult to negotiate prices on packaged tours. For all other options however, you can, depending on your approach, either overspend or negotiate a satisfactory price. A few examples will illustrate.

When pre-booking our accommodation, we typically follow these steps:

- *Research via the web, information on accommodation options, locations, prices, and amenities for our destination. A key site is **www.hotwire.com**.*

- *Still on the web, review the offerings of several travel-discounters, to explore their offerings for the specific dates and locations we want.*

- *Considering amenities and location, narrow our choices to the one or two hotels, B&B's, or pensions that most appeal to us.*

- *Ascertain the travel-discounter's best-price available, consistent with both our lodging choices, and our specific dates.*

- *Google the websites for these particular accommodations; check their on-line booking prices for those dates, and obtain their 1-800 reservations number.*

- *Call, if our target is a hotel in a major chain such as Fairmont, Sheraton, or Best Western, their 1-800 number; check prices through that avenue.*

- *Phone the hotel directly, and politely negotiate for the best rate they will offer, adding that we qualify for "seniors" rates, or belong to an automobile club, or own a particular credit card—whatever may help to reduce the tariff.*

- *Ask to speak to the reservations manager if the reservations clerk is inflexible, or not authorized to negotiate on price, particularly if booking for multiple nights. Begin the process again, asking for the best price.*

The inevitable result from these multiple price inquiries, is that I will then have a range of prices, some much better than others, from which to choose.

Take note ! One price quote may *include* breakfast and/or parking; others may not. Be sure your final decision is based on comparable offerings, suitable to your needs.

....

Always ask as well, if the hotel belongs to *your* Travel-Miles Reward programme.

Many major hotel chains have their own *loyalty programs* which both reward and entice repeat guests to return. They offer a number of incentives from discounted rates, to upgrades, and even free nights.

If you are a senior, often as young as 55, swallow your pride and ask for the senior's rate. If you are employed by government, or another organization that enjoys special rates at a particular establishment, ask for that rate.

If you are flexible on dates, enquire whether the price is reduced on certain days of the week. Weekends frequently cost less than week-days because fewer business travellers book in. The hotel is anxious to fill the rooms. Ask if breakfast is included—it makes a difference to your budgeting.

As a result of years of refining the above approach, I have reached a number of conclusions:

- *Speaking directly with the reservations desk can at times yield the best price.*

  For a five-night stay in Portland, Oregon, with a major hotel chain, our best internet price was $189 per night. A direct call to the hotel yielded, for exactly the same dates, a rate of $129 per night, with a substantial breakfast included.

  During a stay in Prague, friends asked us to arrange hotel accommodations for them, in a well-located three-star hotel. We had a particular hotel in mind for them, since we were familiar with it and its central location. The best daily rate we could find on the internet, among numerous discounters and the hotel's own website, was 130 euros. We decided to stop in at the hotel to speak with the reservations manager. The result—a nightly rate for our friends of 77 euros, with full breakfast. Our small effort saved our friends 53 euros or about $80. Over their three-night stay, this savings of $240, proved to be enough to cover the cost of all their meals for their entire stay.

peter dolezal

- *Belonging to a hotel chain's President's Club, or its equivalent, often results in the 1-800 agent or the reservations clerk trying harder to offer a better deal; even an upgrade to the Executive floor can result in a free breakfast and other benefits which are a boon to the budget.*

- *The Auto-club connection at times yields the best value, with a significant discount on posted rates.*

- *The longer the proposed stay, the better the per-night rate tends to be.*

- *On occasion, the internet route does offer the better price.*

A word of caution. Be prepared for the occasional surprise, particularly when booking on-line. Enhanced photos and flowery descriptions can create perceptions that are not necessarily the real thing.

*Some years ago, we booked on-line, what appeared to be a wonderful, boutique hotel near Hyde Park in London, England. Once we checked in, we quickly learned that our room was a five-floor walk-up to the attic level, via narrow circular stairs. The room itself was about 80 square feet, with no closet, and the bathroom, a miniscule converted closet that you had to back into! The high-volume traffic noise stopped only between 2:00 and 5:00 a.m. Although we laughed about our luxury London loft, the $230 daily price tag was **not** reflective of good value, even in ultra-expensive London. All in all, it was not a successful on-line booking!*

TIP # 29 ..... **Before booking accommodation sight-unseen, avoid being disappointed. Check out what others have to say about it on websites such as *www.tripadvisor.com*.**

Clearly, it is not possible to generalize on any one specific approach as being the best tactic. To realize best-value for each particular situation, you really must be prepared to invest time in investigating each of these options.

For us, booking accommodation using these general guidelines has, over the years, saved us many thousands of dollars on our overall travel budget. ***With equal effort, you can do the same.***

TIP # 30 ..... With a bit of extra up-front effort when making reservations, a traveller can often achieve discounts of 50% or more, on a hotel's posted rack rate.

When booking accommodations in major European destinations, I continue to use the above approach.

I also invest in a copy of Rick Steves' latest travel guide for our specific area of interest. He often recommends charming three-star boutique hotels, which we have found to provide excellent value. Some of these establishments even offer a 10 or 15% discount if you flash his book when you check in. Even after testing against my usual system, we have always found his suggestions hard to beat.

TIP # 31 ..... When planning a visit to another country, the minor investment of purchasing the latest guide book should prove not only very informative and helpful in your planning, but also, should pay for itself many times over through the specific budget-wise tips it offers.

Finding *spur-of-the-moment accommodation* can save you money, be fun, and may contribute to your adventure. If you have a vehicle and are touring for example, Ireland, Scotland, or northern France in a leisurely manner, with no fixed itinerary, stopping to check out an attractive guest house or B&B, may well result in a real deal. When you walk in for a look, the owner knows that you are an instant potential customer. If his establishment is not full, he may well offer you a room at a significant discount, rather than have you leave.

We have found many gems world-wide, by deciding to stay overnight after such unplanned impromptu stops.

Often however, not booking ahead can backfire and cause headaches. A week's tour in Tasmania in busy November is not the time to try this approach.

Nor is it during Oktoberfest, when we arrived without reserved accommodation, in Munich, Germany. We wanted to find somewhere to stay for a few nights. Not only was this impossible at any price, but also, we had to travel another 100 kilometers by train before any rooms were to be found!

Similarly, on arriving in Florence one September, our options were so limited, that we had to settle for an overpriced room whose door handle kept falling off, mould climbed up the shower curtain, and the bidet was so unappealing, that we did not, as was our habit, use it even to chill our wine!

7. HOTEL REWARD PROGRAMS

Just as airlines do, many hotels and hotel chains offer a myriad of reward programs. Personally, I have found most to be not worth the hassle. Generally, they require the accumulation of too many "points" before one earns a free night.

One possible exception can be found through ***www.hotels.com***. Not only will this site give you numerous price and value options for most cities world-wide, but also, it offers a simple reward program that results in a free night after booking a total of 10 nights in any one of

35,000 member hotels. You can even choose your free night in a hotel of a much higher value than you normally book.

Be careful however. Never let your decision be driven simply by a reward program and a value that, at first glance, looks good. Test the value using techniques similar to those previously outlined in this chapter in *Section 6 –Booking Best Value.*

TIP # 32..... **Hotel reward programs may offer value. Do not however, let these incentive programs cause you to ignore a broader assessment of best-value before booking.**

CHAPTER THIRTEEN

LONG-STAY ACCOMMODATION

Summer temperatures when it's winter at home. Ovens that function on Celsius. Right-hand drive vehicles that wander to the wrong side of the road. All part of the experience!

You have the available time, and the urge to get away, but in looking for a particularly *good-value* holiday, are not yet ready to consider renting out or sharing your home through a home-exchange arrangement.

Consider instead the **long-stay** option. It is available virtually anywhere in the world that you may wish to visit or explore in depth. Google *Long Stay Accommodations* for insights.

Self-contained accommodation, known to many as "self-catering" or "holiday lets", can generally be found at rates that you would be hard-pressed to rival, unless you are hostelling. Arrangements can be made for as little as one week; most however, require a minimum commitment of two to four weeks. Suites or apartments are the usual offering. However, unique solutions such as mobile homes, ski chalets, float-homes, villas, and castles are available.

Long-stays are available by private arrangement via the web, or through organized options offered by travel agencies. Various North American Automobile Associations have established a loyal following of long-stay aficionados.

Some preferred long-stay destinations, favoured by North Americans wanting to escape winter's harsh weather include, of course, the southern U.S., but also the Hawaiian Islands, Mexico, Central America,

the naked traveller

Australia, New Zealand, France's Riviera and Provence, Portugal's Algarve, Spain's Costa del Sol, and the Adriatic region. A multitude of new locations is being added annually, as our population ages and flocks to sunnier climes.

Through our provincial auto club, the BCAA, my wife and I have, over the years, taken advantage of several of their long-stay offerings, each for four-to-six-week periods. These winter getaways have proven to be among our least expensive travels. For us, the bonus has always been the very real opportunity to live like a local.

We have rarely paid more than $2,500 per person for a four-week stay, including air fare, even on the French Riviera. The accommodation has always been exactly as advertised, and particularly important to us because we prefer to not rent a vehicle, centrally located in the community.

The winter weather in both the south of France and Portugal ranged from 12 to 22 degrees Celsius; not hot, but certainly warmer than at home and very comfortable, ideally suited to hiking and sightseeing.

On several other occasions, we have independently arranged long-stay vacations, in privately-owned apartments, in both Mexico and Australia. Again, we found that the overall costs represented superb values.

When we returned home after five and six-week stays in Mexico for example, our vacation "post-mortem" consistently indicated that our entire trip costs amounted to only about $1,000 to $2,000 more than had we stayed at home, with our normal spending pattern!

Our Australia long-stay vacation apartment proved to be more costly. Compared to local hotel and resort options however, it again provided excellent value.

....

During their year-long sabbatical in Europe, friends decided to spend the month of December in Portugal. They found a large, well-furnished house, complete with resident caretaker on the property. The letdown? No central heating. The good news? A rental cost of only $1,200 for the month. The bonus? Their family, for the cost of airfare only, was able to join them for two weeks over Christmas.

You may find the following sites useful for checking out long-stay options:

- *www.vrbo.com*
- *www.homeaway.com*
- *www.ownersdirect.com*
- *www.resortquest.com*
- *www.zonder.com*

TIP # 33 ..... If you are debt-free at home, and have the time, a long-stay vacation rental, even in an exotic location, can provide a terrific holiday value, at very modest incremental cost over what you might spend by staying home!

CHAPTER FOURTEEN

HOME EXCHANGE

Would you jump at the chance to "live" in an ancient farm-house in rural France? Or an exclusive seaside apartment on Australia's Gold Coast? Or perhaps a cozy, timbered home high in the Swiss Alps?

The practice of **home-exchange** has existed for decades. In recent years, it has become mainstream, rocketing in popularity. This budget-wise option is perfect for you if you truly wish, for a period of time, to be absorbed into the day-to-day life of a distant community, and to experience its culture like a true local. What better holiday or sabbatical for you and your family, than free accommodation in a location you have long wanted to visit?

As with any successful travel venture however, doing your advance homework is key.

Googling **Home Exchanges** will yield hundreds of choices worldwide. Most websites require a modest membership fee. This will open the door to all of that site's services, including descriptive listings and contact details, for potential home-exchanges.

As a starting point, key sites include:

- *www.craigslist.com*
- *www.homeexchange.com*
- *www.exchangehomes.org*
- *www.anotherhome.com*

- *www.intervac.com*

Craigslist is a free site. All the others charge a modest fee.

At first glance, the home-exchange process may appear somewhat overwhelming, like trying to put together an intricate jigsaw puzzle.

You are looking for a family or a couple, more or less like yourselves, who live in a distant city, or even country, and who *may* wish to occupy your home at *exactly* the same time that you wish to inhabit theirs.

You are faced with an initial major decision. Do you:

- List your home on the exchange, hoping for a positive response?
- Simply explore current offerings, in an effort to locate a home in a destination that suits your schedule and travel budget?

As a first-timer, you may prefer the latter option. You have a destination in mind, and you know when you would prefer to travel.

Contact several *listers* at your destination-of-choice. Explore their interest in exchanging homes with you.

Once you receive a positive response, the careful detailed work and planning begin in earnest. You have specific needs, and a wish list. So does the other party. Do the two match or complement one another?

If you have a non-smoking home in North America, you are not likely to want to exchange homes with a family of smokers, even if the dates match perfectly. If you are allergic to animal dander, you will want to avoid pet-friendly homes. If you have mobility issues, you may not want that heritage multi-level home.

Take your time. Be sure that the exchange upon which you eventually settle, is what *you* want and need. After all, once you accept it, this will be your *home* for the agreed length of time.

One of our favourite "homes" was a 120-year old, low-ceilinged stone cottage in rural France. Although charming, it had its quirks. There wasn't a single comfortable chair; we needed a degree in rocket science to operate the miniature washing machine; and the single low-wattage lamp in the sitting room provided a challenge for reading. But the ambience of the garden, and the magical village with its twice-weekly markets and friendly people, more than compensated for these shortcomings.

Often included in home-exchanges is the use of one another's personal property, items such as vehicles, bicycles, kayaks, or snowmobiles. You may agree to exchange certain services such as feeding their goats, in exchange for weeding your garden. Some well-organized and considerate home-exchangers provide maps and information on local attractions and services, as well as the name of a neighbour willing to help out if necessary.

Unless you particularly enjoy the challenge of this type of quest, the effort involved in finding that *perfect* match may not be worthwhile if you are planning only a very brief one-week stopover. On the other hand, if you are intending a sojourn of a month or more, this could be an ideal solution for you. It will certainly stretch your travel-dollar, saving you significantly on accommodation costs.

....

Should you decide to pursue a home-exchange, it is crucial that you include a few vital details in your all-important check-list:

- Ensure that *your* home-insurance policy will cover any normal insured risk if strangers occupy your home for an extended period. If not, add the necessary rider.
- If use of your vehicle is part of the exchange, review your car insurance policy. Be particularly aware of the consequence to your future premiums, should your visitor have an accident while driving your vehicle. If necessary, add extra insurance to protect yourself from that risk. Have the vehicle serviced to ensure that it is left in top condition.

- Ask a few key questions of your home-exchange *host*. Be sure that both the home, and any vehicles to which you are given access, are also sufficiently insured before your arrival.

....

After that first successful home-exchange experience, many of us become instant converts, barely home again before we avidly begin researching our next home-away-from-home adventure.

If you find yourself eager to try more home-exchanges, then perhaps it's time to consider registering *your* home on a home-exchange website. Again, do your homework. For instance:

- Do you want only North American exposure, or international?

- What should your listing look like, and what should it include?

Detailed information is what "sells" your home to others. Examine other listings. Which ones appeal to you? Why do they do so? Use a similar format, adapted to your specific situation.

- Are you clear about *your* expectations? If your wish is to host only non-smokers, no pets, and no children under 12 years of age, make that very clear at the outset.

*A number of our acquaintances regularly participate in home exchanges. Extremely satisfied with their experiences, **all** have reported that they now would not consider any other mode of accommodation, when planning a long-stay getaway.*

TIP # 34 ..... Considering a home-exchange for an extended holiday or sabbatical, is well-worthwhile, if you have the patience to do your homework, and if you take great care in the selection process.

CHAPTER FIFTEEN

VACATION TIMESHARES

A free week for two in a new condo development; a free cruise; free car rental or dinner for two—all yours, if you will both simply sit through a brief presentation.

Most of us have experienced a sales pitch along these lines—all designed to capture our interest in purchasing a timeshare when our defenses are at their lowest—while we are on vacation.

There are those who have the notion that owning a timeshare is a great investment that significantly reduces the cost of future holidays, while at the same time appreciating, due to the property's underlying value. Is this perception correct?

With very few exceptions, the answer is NO!

In Puerto Vallarta, we became acquainted with two couples from Canada who, in return for a $100 dinner voucher, decided to attend a timeshare presentation. Gaye refused to go; she becomes irritated with the high-pressure sales-pitch into which such sessions invariably degenerate.

The next day we learned that one of the couples had, for $18,000, committed to a one- week timeshare. They excitedly celebrated their good fortune.

The other couple had held back, wanting to think through the pros and cons of such an investment. Some days later however, urged on by their exuberant friends, they returned a second time to sit through the presentation.

Despite the second sales-pitch, they remained firm that it was too much money for them to commit at that time. Sensing that it was more a financial issue than a basic unwillingness to buy, the salesman caught them on their way out the door. He offered them the same unit, for $12,000. This was $6,000 less than their friends had paid only days before!

The couple, shocked by the offer, still refused. They shared with their friends this latest chapter in the saga. The friends, absolutely livid, tried to back out of their obligation. Unfortunately, the grace period for cancelling had passed, and they were legally bound!

This unfortunate incident, not uncommon, illustrates both the high marketing costs and the astronomical margin of profit, built into new-timeshare prices.

These particular units in Mexico would have cost at most, $50,000 each to build. Yet, at $18,000 per week, they were being marketed at almost $1 million, on a 52-week, sold-out basis!

TIP # 35 ...... **New timeshares are almost always a *depreciating* asset. They are often resold for a fraction of their original cost. Never view a *new* timeshare purchase as an investment for capital appreciation!**

It is wise to keep in mind as well, that once you *do* invest in a unit, the future cost of owning can be significant.

Many owners choose to place their timeshare unit in a rental pool. Even so, net proceeds are seldom more than 40% of the actual rent charged.

The annual maintenance fee, whether you use the unit or not, can be between $500 and $1,000 per ownership week. When you do occupy the unit, there is often an *additional* fee for housekeeping and cleaning.

Our attraction to timeshares generally occurs when we are in a very happy, carefree, and upbeat mood in the midst of our vacation. This makes us particularly vulnerable to the lure of free gifts, excursions or meals, and to the ensuing well-honed sales-pitch.

The next time the lure is dangled before your eyes, detour first to the nearest internet café. Go on line and google "Timeshare Sales". You may be shocked to find hundreds of timeshares offered on the *resale* market for one quarter, or even less, their original purchase price! You may even find resales available in the very locale, in which you are now being tempted to buy *new*.

There are many reasons for resales. Health issues have an impact. The more likely reason however, is economics. Those selling their unit often do so, desperate to escape the high annual fee which they must pay - whether or not they use their allocated time period.

> **TIP # 36 ..... If you are determined to own a timeshare, you owe it to yourself to fully investigate the re-sale market, prior to making a purchase commitment.**

....

Having outlined the negative aspects of *new-timeshare* ownership, it is fair to say that if one buys carefully on the **resale** market, time-shares *can* prove to be good value.

A visit to ***www.ebay.com*** will yield hundreds of *resale timeshares* on offer, usually at a fraction of their original purchase price.

If buying for the first time, you may be wise to look for units offered by experienced timeshare sellers. They are easily identified because they normally have multiple units available for sale. Most of these units are offered through on-line auctions.

Don't jump into the bidding too quickly. Watch to see how the system works. If you miss a few opportunities, don't worry; there are many more to be found.

If you do purchase a timeshare, never choose really *cheap* off-season weeks. There is always a reason for the unusually low price. These weeks are virtually worthless as investments, unless you plan to use them yourself. You will soon discover that the ability to trade, rent, or sell your weeks is close to a mission-impossible.

*Friends in Victoria have, over the years, bought three separate timeshare weeks, in three different complexes in Hawaii—all on the **resale** market. They paid between $3,000 and $4,000 per week, a small fraction of the original purchase price. They also wisely chose to buy their timeshares in the form of **vacation points**, which can be traded for stays in hundreds of different holiday complexes, world-wide.*

Because of the relative value of their highly-desirable Hawaiian locations, our friends are often able to trade their three weeks of Hawaiian vacation points, for up to six weeks of luxury accommodation elsewhere in the U.S., Mexico, Central America, and even Europe. Although they tend to use their full entitlement each year, they are permitted to carry forward any unused points, to the following year. This enables them to plan longer vacations in a subsequent year.

For this couple, investing in *resale timeshares* has worked out very well. In fact, should they eventually decide to resell their rights, they may, unlike many others, actually make a profit on their original investment.

The lesson for would-be, budget-wise timeshare-owners is:

- Generally, *resale* purchases represent best, and sometimes great, value;

- High-value locations, such as Hawaii, are best;

- Highly exchangeable units in popular destinations offer better investment value;

- Units in premium high-season weeks are most desirable;

- The total annual *holding* cost must be factored in to your ownership cost;

- Regular use of your entitlement ensures greater value to the owner.

TIP # 37..... **Before purchasing a timeshare, new or resale, calculate the projected *total* cost of ownership, over a set number of years. Compare that to the cost of renting first-class accommodation over the same period. If the numbers make sense to you, then consider buying. But buy smart – buy resale!**

FRACTIONAL OWNERSHIP

An interesting and more recent development is the availability of *fractional-ownership* interests which may be purchased in *real property assets.* Google **Fractional Ownership** for information on the many forms such ownership interests take, in many locations.

Fractional ownership divides a property's title into more affordable segments than full ownership of the property. It also matches a purchaser's ownership allotment to his actual occupancy entitlement. Typically, a quarter-ownership interest for example, will give the purchaser one week of use monthly, with the week rotating through the calendar each year to even out every owner's access to desirable weeks such as Christmas or Spring Break. Other fractional ownerships on the other hand, may designate specific fixed periods for use.

Fractional ownerships are typically sold as 1/12, 1/10, or 1/4 interest, but other variations exist.

The advantage of fractional ownership over timeshare ownership is that with fractional ownership you actually receive title to your share of the asset. With a timeshare you receive only a right to the *use* of a property for a specific week or weeks during the year.

This distinction tends to give fractional ownership a big advantage in terms of potential value-appreciation over time. As the value of the underlying property asset increases, theoretically at least, so does that of your fractional ownership share. Obviously, to capitalize on this advantage, saleability is key. Fractional ownership in the resort community of Whistler, British Columbia for instance, is likely to be a solid long-term investment. Relative to timeshare interests, it should also be much easier to sell.

Despite this key advantage, fractional ownership tends on the whole, to be less expensive when calculated on a per-week basis, than is the case with acquiring a timeshare interest. The one downside is that usually, you have to purchase a minimum 1/12 to 1/4 interest in the property. Your initial financial commitment is much greater therefore, than the purchase of a timeshare interest of one or two weeks.

TIP # 38.... If considering the purchase of a costly time-share, examine the fractional ownership option as a possible alternative.

CHAPTER SIXTEEN

THE "SNOWBIRD" ESCAPE

How often have you escaped winter for a few weeks, to an idyllic sunny location, and enviously encountered snowbirds, nesting for another three months or more, in either their own or rental accommodation?

Appealing? You bet it is!

It is particularly attractive for the legions of younger retirees who, having both the time and the desire to escape winter's challenges, prefer to swing a golf club than a snow shovel, and to trade long-johns for shorts.

1. THE RENTAL OPTION

Clarify your needs. Do you want:

- Peace and quiet, or a very social setting?
- Adults-only, or family-oriented?
- Golf? Hiking? Swimming? Nothing?
- Desert, mountain, beach or urban setting?

Renting is an easy-to-arrange, low-risk means of exploring whether an extended absence from home has appeal. It also provides an opportunity to shop around, trying different destinations and accommodation options, before locking in to a specific long-term solution.

The web provides access to numerous sites which offer long-term, monthly rental rates on suites, condos, townhomes, modular homes and houses, throughout the world. Again, *www.VRBO.com*, is an excellent website to start your exploration of options.

Closer to home, in sunny, southern U.S. locales such as Florida, Arizona, Texas, and California, prices as low as $600 per month, can be found.

More distant options are offered throughout the Caribbean area, in for example, Mexico, Belize, Costa Rica, and Panama, and yet further afield, in Hawaii, New Zealand, and Australia.

If a tropical setting is not among your requirements, don't ignore the possibilities of southern Portugal, France, Spain, Italy and the Adriatic. All exude charm and, even in winter, enjoy many sunny days and moderate temperatures.

Remember, the higher cost of travel to the more distant locales becomes more affordable when spread over the three or four-month period of your stay. Those with little or no debt at home, can enjoy extended winter absences for virtually the same cost, as were they to remain shivering at home all winter.

2. THE OWNERSHIP OPTION

Unlike timeshare ownership, which usually involves a depreciating asset, the careful purchase of a *vacation home* in a sunny clime, *can* be an excellent long-term investment.

Always keep in mind the three key rules of investing in real estate, whether domestic or foreign: Location, location, location!

When investing in foreign real estate, add these few extra precautions to your *normal due diligence* process:

- Research the local *title-ownership rules* and restrictions. Read the fine print; ensure that they make sense. Straightforward in some countries, they are less so in others, as in Mexico. Usually the more complicated the system, the greater the legal fees, and the potential for future problems.

- Research the *income-tax consequences*, should you subsequently decide to sell the property.

- Research the *residency laws* at your proposed ownership-destination. Is there a maximum time-limit for each stay?

- Understand the rules for attaining *permanent residency*, should you eventually wish to become a permanent resident of that country.

- Ascertain the *rental potential* of the accommodation, and the tax consequences of renting. You may decide to not use the unit for some time. Can you find a reliable rental agent? How much will he charge to manage your property?

- Determine the *realistic* annual operating and maintenance costs of ownership. Can you comfortably afford that cost?

- Research the quality of *health care*, its accessibility, and its cost. Do you qualify to purchase out-of-country health insurance? Would it make sense to do so?

- Satisfy yourself with respect to the *political stability* of your target country.

- Make decisions relevant to issues concerning your *existing home*. Rent it? Sell it? Leave it vacant for your periodic use? What are the insurance issues?

If you are comfortable with the answers to these questions, and others specific to *your* situation, by all means consider a purchase. But don't jump in too quickly—test the waters first!

Try the rental route for at least the first year. Satisfy yourself that a long-term interest in that location does have year-round appeal and make sense for you. While renting, check out the local real estate market. Confer with a reliable local lawyer. Discuss your plans with other foreign owners. Do your homework, *before* committing to a purchase!

IF one takes a long-term view, most real estate investments turn out well. Do not expect however, to make money if you buy, and then, a short year or two later, conclude that it was the wrong decision. Reselling in the shorter term, will almost always *cost* you, in some cases a great deal of money.

3. PERMANENT RESIDENCY IN PARADISE

You rented for one or two winters in that idyllic location. You think you are ready to purchase a residence. You are seriously considering making it your permanent home.

Some facts are in your favour. The living costs are much lower than at home. You can buy a better home, on or near a beach or golf course, for less than you can sell your home in North America. Among other requirements, you meet the country's minimum income or capital requirements, which are necessary for you to achieve permanent residency.

Why hesitate? Why not take the plunge, and go for it?

You do not yet have enough information, to minimize the considerable commitment and risk associated with such a life-altering decision.

What other factors deserve serious consideration?

- Visit a knowledgeable accountant at home. Are you comfortable with the specific *tax and pension consequences* of becoming a non-resident? What is the process for reversing your decision, should you later wish to return?

- Call your *health care* provider. How long will your coverage continue? Can it be reinstated, should you decide to return one day? Do you require additional out-of-country coverage, and at what cost?

- Carefully confirm that you meet *all* of the *residency require-ments* for your target country. What are its taxation rules regarding your pension and investment income? Can you work part-time, should you wish to do so?

- Make the necessary decisions regarding your present home.

- Finally, discuss your plans with immediate family, and others to whom you are particularly close. Are you satisfied that family connections can remain stable and comfortable for everyone, should you make a move? How often can they visit you, or you them?

With diligent effort you should be able to resolve all of these issues to your satisfaction. North Americans are noted for their flexibility and adaptability.

For peace of mind however, before selling your North American holdings and committing to a *permanent* relocation, one further act of *due diligence* is advisable.

Visit this dream-come-true-location again. But *don't follow your usual pattern*. This time visit during the off-season summer months, rather than in winter, which you already know you love. Your winter paradise may become a very uncomfortable, humid, scorching-hot, or mosquito-infested purgatory in June, July and August. During these periods it could be subject to savage tropical storms. How well will you adapt to any or all of these off-season realities?

If you truly have done your homework, and are convinced that a permanent move is, for you, a sound economic and lifestyle decision - **GO FOR IT**!

....

Decision made. Snowbird nest is purchased. You feel like you've won the lottery. You celebrate your good fortune. Many friends and relatives plan to visit. Life is good!

We have met in Mexico, a number of North American and European expats, who having taken up permanent residency, remain delighted with their decision years after relocating. Favourite communities seem to be Lake Chapala, San Miguel de Allende, San Jose del Cabo, and Cabo San Lucas, La Paz, Mazatlan, and Puerto Vallarta.

Countries such as Panama, Belize, Costa Rica, Spain and Malaysia welcome foreigners, going to great lengths to make it relatively easy for them to become full-time residents.

The U.S., and most European countries, generally restrict long-stays to no more than six months in any one year. Permanent residency is usually possible only under very specific circumstances, primarily work-related. If such is the case at your target destination, include in your financial planning, the cost of extended travel away from your new home every six months. In the final analysis, you may well conclude that pursuing a long-term *rental* option is your best or perhaps, only solution.

TIP # 39 ...... Becoming either a regular *snowbird*, or a permanent resident in another country is a major decision. Be sure to perform the necessary due diligence, *prior* to making long-term commitments, particularly those involving the purchase of real estate.

....

CHAPTER SEVENTEEN

TRAVEL ON THE CHEAP

If you are old enough, you may recall the travel guides of the 1960's and 70's with titles such as "Europe on $10 a Day". Those days are long gone. Equally gone however, are the $10,000-a-year salaries, which represented very good income at that time.

It is still possible today to travel on a very reasonable budget, *if* you firmly decide to do so, and remain committed to your objective. Although I have already touched on a few effective techniques, such as those used by our nephew during his $40-per-day, four-month travels, let me now elaborate in some detail.

1. AIR TRAVEL COSTS

It *does* pay to **shop around** for the best deal. Getting to and from your destination can consume a significant portion of your overall travel budget. A few reminders:

- Fly free, using reward-miles if you have them, particularly for the longer, more expensive flights;

- Be as flexible as possible on travel dates, to obtain the best-possible prices;

- If possible, book your travel during fringe, or off-season, periods;

- Comparison-shop the cost of charter versus regular flights;

- Research the growing number of discount carriers world-wide, such as Sky Air and Ryanair; they may fly to your destination. Among others, check out the following websites:

- *www.wegolo.com*
- *www.whichbudget.com*
- *www.hotwire.com*

Important to keep in mind, if you are in a position to enjoy longer holidays, is that ***the longer your vacation, the less the pro-rated, daily cost of your flight***. If your ticket costs $1,000 and you are away for one week, the *per diem* cost of your flight is $143. If you extend your trip to 28 days, as with a long-stay booking, your air-cost reduces to a very modest $36 per day!

Friends of ours, bound for a two-week visit to Paris, booked ten days ahead, on a discount carrier. Each round-trip fare from Vancouver cost them only $650, including all taxes. When I comparison-shopped online, on the same day they purchased their tickets, the best alternate price I could find on any other airline, amounted to $1,350 per person, more than twice what our friends paid!

TIP # 40 ..... Because air fare is such a large part of your overall travel cost, you will reap a significant return, on any extra effort you invest in finding the best possible ticket price.

Be warned however. When booking a *discount carrier*, recognize that their low-cost structure makes them much more vulnerable to sudden financial collapse than is a well-established, major carrier.

The carrier our friends chose for their Paris trip was Zoom Airlines, a Canadian company which had successfully operated for five years. Several months after their comfortable and inexpensive trip, this airline suddenly ceased operations, due to insolvency. Hundreds of passengers were left stranded. Those who had not paid for their ticket by credit card, were out of pocket for the full amount they had spent on their Zoom tickets.

> **TIP # 41 ..... In order to protect your investment, always pay for your tickets with a credit card, which will reimburse you in the event of failure of the carrier.**

---

2. PACKAGE DEALS

Whether you are escaping to a sunny location in winter, or planning a once-in-a-lifetime jaunt to Prague, Panama, or Perth, it always pays to research the costs and benefits of travel *packages*. Generally included are transportation, accommodation, transfers, and occasionally, extras such as excursions, entertainment, and partial or even full, meal plans.

Due to the high volume of travellers they attract, consolidators, charter companies, travel agencies, or air carriers have far greater purchasing power, than do you, as an individual.

The end-result is that, even after the tour-operator adds in his profit margin, *your* total cost may well be less than anything you can arrange independently.

Dramatic instances of such bargains exist world-wide; for example, in packaged excursions to London, England - one of the world's most expensive destinations, particularly for the budget-minded. Charter carriers offer "bundled" trips to London, for one to two-week holidays. These include very acceptable accommodation, whether at a single locale for your entire stay, or a series of locations during a tour. The *entire* cost is often less than one-half that of the individually-listed components one would typically have to pay, in making his own arrangements.

The ultimate packaged vacation, particularly appealing to families, is the **all-inclusive** stay. This usually covers flight, transfers, room, meals, activities, and in some cases, extras such as beverages. Prices will vary with the "star" rating of the accommodation you select. The appeal is that not only is the planning done for you, but also, with the inclusion of these basic features, your overall trip cost becomes almost totally predictable.

....

When an opportunity arises to *combine* the benefits of this all-inclusive option with a **last-minute** offering, you may be amazed at the deals available to you.

A little time and effort invested in research can result in huge budget-wise dividends.

*I googled **Last Minute Travel**. Within seconds, I was bombarded by pages of offers. Using as my focus, travel from Vancouver, BC to Mexico's resort areas, I found dozens of all-inclusive packages, departing within the next two weeks. Several all-inclusive, one-week stays in three-star hotels were priced at less than $500 per person (excluding taxes). Two-week options were priced from $700 per person.*

These bargains were undoubtedly influenced by the fact that my price inquiry occurred in October, during the fringe season in Mexico.

Regardless of the time of year however, it pays to check out the potential for savings. ***You want to stretch that travel-dollar until it squeals!***

TIP # 42 ..... All-inclusive travel packages, particularly when booked off-season as last minute travel, can result in significant savings. The *total* cost of your trip will often be less than you might have otherwise paid, for the normal economy airfare alone.

---

3. TRAVEL LIKE A LOCAL

If prepared to adapt your expectations and embrace local customs, you can drastically reduce the cost of your trip.

I earlier referred to friends who every winter, spend four or five months in Zihuatanejo, Mexico, for no more than it would cost them to stay at home. What I failed to mention, is that their total monthly expenses average no more than $1,000!

How do they manage? Following a simple formula, they:

- Arrange the cheapest flight possible;
- Negotiate accommodation in a small family-run apartment-hotel, frequented more by Mexican, than North American tourists. Their choice is clean and air-conditioned; has a kitchen, but no view;
- Shop in local markets; dine alfresco, eating delectable meals they create from local recipes and produce;
- Eat out rarely, perhaps twice a week, in local neighbourhood restaurants, off the tourist track;
- Pack picnic lunches in a thermal cooler, for daily beach excursions;
- Use only local bus transportation;
- Immerse themselves in the culture, developing friendships

with local families, and becoming involved in volunteer work in the community. This, in turn, has led to frequent, inexpensive outings with locals—fishing trips, family celebrations, cooking and language lessons, and day trips to new discoveries far off the tourist track.

We have visited their miniscule apartment, very centrally located, with a tiny but serviceable kitchen, and its own bathroom. Their little hotel complex has a modest pool, and the bonus - a large covered rooftop deck where residents can socialize, and even barbecue, while sipping Margaritas and enjoying magnificent sunsets over the Pacific Ocean.

This apartment costs our friends a grand total of $500 per month! Almost unbelievable, but true.

More amazing is that, for their total monthly outlay of $1,000, our friends enjoy the *same* spectacular weather, ambience, beaches, ocean, and fresh seafood, that other tourist couples do, at up to five times the cost!

Similar opportunities abound world-wide, in for instance Southeast Asia, much of Central America, and the former Eastern-Block countries of Europe. More familiar with bargain offerings in Mexico and Australia, we continue to stretch our horizons as we search out new locales.

You too can enjoy an equally inexpensive holiday. The rules are simple - **be willing to do your homework, and travel, live, and eat like a local!**

....

For us, travelling like a local has proven successful time and again, even in Europe.

We often visit my large extended family near Prague, in the Czech Republic. We are always amazed by the frequent, incredibly

109

inexpensive holidays that an aunt and uncle have enjoyed, all over Europe.

They book their vacations through local travel agents, opting for one or two-week excursions. They always choose "packaged tours" with a combination of charter bus and plane travel. Usually included in the package is at least half-board, generally two meals a day. Accommodation is usually in two, and at times three-star hotels, often with a private bathroom.

As a result of their budget-wise approach, they have, with extremely limited resources, managed to explore, among others, Spain, Cyprus, Sardinia, Germany, Austria, Hungary, France and Greece.

During each of these tours, they have never gone over their limited pre-determined budget of roughly $500 per person in local currency.

....

What is the secret? Why can we North Americans not do the same?

We can, but it does not come easily. We tend to be somewhat spoiled, often expecting our travel comforts to match those at home.

If we Google the same destinations to which my aunt and uncle travel, we will find numerous English-language sites offering countless options. *But,* they will be offered by North American tour providers, at North American prices. In other words, no bargain!

To travel like a European local, try this. First and foremost, jettison your pre-conceived misperceptions, and alter your expectations.

Book only your initial flight and perhaps the first night or two of accommodation, in your first central destination, such as Prague, Warsaw, or Budapest. Stay there a few nights. Explore the city. While there, wander into a local travel agency. Most agents are multi-lingual and speak excellent English. Ask about current, last-minute excursions to other European locales in which you are interested.

The result? You may be offered the same tours, at the same prices, that my aunt and uncle have enjoyed for years. If you are a student or retiree, with a carefree calendar, you could travel around Europe almost continuously, for less than $500 per week.

Another illustration: *This same aunt and uncle recently returned from eight days in a spa resort, in the Tatra Mountains of northern Slovakia. They travelled by bus, and had a comfortable room with a private bath. All meals were provided **and**, they each received vouchers for thirteen individual therapeutic treatments. The total cost? 6,000 korunas each, about $350! They returned home well-fed, toned, tanned and refreshed, with hardly a dent in their bank balance.*

One proviso however. You *are* travelling like a local to all of these destinations. While the tour bus may well have a guide, all of his commentary will be in the local language, perfect for 95% of his passengers, whether Czech, Slovak, Polish, Hungarian or other regional nationality. *You* may miss out on the incomprehensible narration, although many guides will make *some* effort to answer your questions in English. Carrying a guide book on the area, as well as a phrasebook, is always worthwhile. *You* will decide if the huge savings are worth this minor inconvenience.

....

Why, if bargains such as these are so readily available in much of Europe, can they not be pre-purchased in North America? They *are* available, but with significant extra effort.

If you speak the country's language, use that skill. Google travel options in that language. You may find the same deals as would a local. A significant problem however, is that even when you do find an attractive offer, many operators will not accept a North American credit card, whether by phone or online. If you are fortunate enough to have a friend or relative who resides in Europe, they may be able on your behalf, to book and pay for the trip you have chosen.

Unfortunately, few North Americans possess the necessary language skills. The minute we begin our search in English, we will be faced with "western" solutions and prices.

....

These spectacular deals are often available *only* within the borders of the specific countries. Tour operators, transportation companies, hotels, and resorts must price their products at an economic, afford-able level for the local population.

In the former eastern-block countries, average incomes are climb-ing steadily. They tend to hover however, at one-third to one-half the wage levels of Western Europe or North America. Local travel indus-try providers must make their products affordable for their *local* con-sumer. Hence the bargains, for savvy North Americans and Western Europeans.

While the best deals can be found in Eastern Europe, and in other developing economies world-wide, bargains *for locals* do exist even in more expensive destinations such as England, France and Germany.

Consider this: Fly for instance, into London, Amsterdam or Frankfurt. *Once there*, book your connection via a discount carrier, to another European city. You may choose a flight to Rome, Lisbon or perhaps Athens, for less than $100. Had you booked the same itinerary from home, whether with a major North American or European airline, you probably would have doubled your cost of reaching your ultimate des-tination.

In Portugal, over fresh-from-the-sea lunches of grilled sardines or octopus, we frequently compared experiences with U.K. citizens, who had "popped over" to the Algarve for a long weekend.

How, we wondered, could so many average, middle-class individuals afford to do so? They simply booked with discount tour operators, or air carriers, at incredibly low, often last-minute "sell-off" prices.

Earlier, I referred to friends who flew round-trip to Paris from Vancouver, for about $650 each, with a discount charter operator. They planned to continue their journey with a flight from Paris to Marseille.

From home they googled for flight information. They were shocked to find the lowest price at about $1,000 per person, greater than the cost of their trans-Atlantic flight. Because they also speak French, they then googled the French site. Lo and behold, the price had miraculously dropped to $200 per person, on precisely the same flight which they had previously researched. They booked the French option!

TIP # 43..... **If you have the patience to seek them out, tremendous travel bargains *do* exist, particularly if you are prepared to adapt, and travel or stay like a local, once you reach your destination.**

---

4. ACCOMMODATION SAVINGS

a) Couch Surfing

Yes, other than flopping in an airport, bus terminal or train station, you really can sleep for free, and still have a roof over your head.

You may encounter a few surprises, but if you are adventurous, or broke, try googling ***www.couchsurfing.ca***.

This website, founded in 2003, provides a bed-for-the-night social network that promotes free intercultural experiences. The service is free and is represented in over 40,000 cities and towns world-wide. This site is fast approaching one million members. It connects travellers to equally adventurous, like-minded individuals who are willing to share their homes with strangers, without charge.

Popular mainly with the younger set who have little choice but to travel cheap, *couch-surfing* has a huge and growing following. If your yen for travel outstrips your pocket-book, try this approach, and save!

b) Hostels

Hostels are to be found almost everywhere. Europe alone boasts well over 2,000 of them. They range in price from a low of $5 per night to $50 and more, for those with private rooms. Next to couch-surfing, tenting or sleeping on a park bench, this mode of accommodation will impact your budget the least. Check out ***www.hihostels.com***.

c) Other Unique Solutions

If you are not into hostelling solutions, check out other budget accommodations, such as a YM or YWCA, a monastery, a university dorm, or even a converted prison!

In Hong Kong, we enjoyed wonderful, water-view, private accommodation in a huge YWCA, only steps from the world-famous top-end-of-the-scale Peninsula Hotel. At about $140 per night, our accommodation was not cheap but, given its quality and location, was definitely a local bargain.

Friends visiting New York City chose to stay in a centrally-located downtown Y. At about the same price of $140 per night, they found it to be by far, the best value available.

In many European cities, monasteries and convents, well-located, are eager to subsidize their existence by welcoming travellers at incredibly modest rates. Accommodation, though at times very spartan, can be had for as little as $50 per room, per night. One such convent in Rome, close to the main railway station, is an oasis of tranquility in the hubbub of the city centre.

A writer friend, sitting in the convent's peaceful little courtyard, with only birds for company, wrote prodigiously, producing volumes during her one-week stay.

d) Budget Chains

In many corners of the world you will find budget-priced, no frills, chain hotels such as *Ibis, Formule 1 and Etap.* The rooms are often tiny, but lack little. Quality, service and amenities are predictable from place to place; and most important, the price is right.

e) One and Two-Star Solutions

If all you need is a clean bed in an expensive city, one option is to choose a one or two-star hotel, much cheaper than a three-star at twice the price or more. Even in Paris, it is still possible to find a double room in a good location at around $75 per night. Be sure, at this rate, that your room isn't above an all-night bar, or facing onto a very noisy street.

TIP # 44 ..... Almost everywhere you travel, you will find accommodation solutions that will suit *your* budget.

---

5. EATING ON THE CHEAP

As with accommodations, you can while travelling, spend very little, or a great deal, on food.

If you are settled into a long-stay apartment with your own kitchen facilities, or you've opted for an all-inclusive solution, the cost of your meals should be easy to manage and control.

Otherwise, be creative. Lunch-time gourmet picnics on a park bench can be had for very little, even in Europe. For a simple but filling meal, search out stand-up food counters which can be found in most European city centres. Local office workers eat there, precisely because they are a bargain.

A street vendor's sausage-on-a-bun, or wurst with mustard and rye bread, is so tasty, filling and cheap, that I could eat them for both lunch and dinner.

Of course, options such as the big "M", KFC, and Domino's Pizza now abound everywhere, although they are rarely cheaper than at home, and can at times cost more.

If, on your budget, you can afford to try a local restaurant, search out a small, family-owned eatery that is off the tourist radar. You will in most cases, not only save significantly, but also enjoy a memorable cultural experience.

On a quiet side street in Rio de Janeiro, Brazil, the aromas of home-cooking drew us into a tiny Italian restaurant. No English was spoken, and we soon realized we were the only tourists in the room. The meal was outstanding, and the price—less than we had paid earlier for a light lunch on the beach. Over the course of a week we returned several times to "our" special find.

TIP # 45..... Meals can be budget-breakers or great bargains. If you plan *how* you eat, you can eat well and still stay within tight food budgets.

CHAPTER EIGHTEEN

THE EUROPEAN SPA EXPERIENCE

If you have enjoyed the experience of a North American *spa treatment*, prepare yourself for a unique treat in continental Europe. For hundreds of years, in eastern European countries such as the Czech Republic, Slovakia, Germany, Poland and Hungary, spas have provided their citizens with both recreation, and therapy for a wide range of ailments.

Earlier I referred to an all-inclusive spa resort in the Tatra Mountains of Slovakia. Such bargains abound throughout these countries, but again, *only* if you book them as a local resident. As a foreigner you can enjoy them, but you will undoubtedly pay a much greater price.

Unlike most spa resorts as we know them in North America, those in Eastern Europe are regarded as an integral part of each country's health-care system. Hundreds of years ago, the benefits of thermal waters, fresh air and exercise were discovered. As a result, many spas were eventually established, particularly in the 19th and 20th centuries, to treat those suffering from almost any illness.

Today, in many countries in Europe, if a doctor believes that a patient's arthritis, stress level, psoriasis, digestive or other problem, might benefit from a spa treatment, one or two-week courses of treatments may be *prescribed*. If you are the local patient who warrants such treatment, you will enjoy all the benefits, including room and board, at absolutely no cost to yourself, for the entire period.

At these spas, physicians, technicians, and nurses will examine you, and prescribe a specific regimen of treatments. These may include hikes, swims, regular or underwater massages, mineral baths, body scrubs, body wraps, and often, dietary regimens of various foods and mineral waters.

Modern "needs" and new technologies have crept in. Anti-aging and cosmetic surgery clinics are now found, adjoining traditional spas in many locations, to treat a new generation of "fountain-of-youth" seekers.

Even without a medical referral, the public-at-large, including the tourist, can also enjoy the benefits of these spas. You will be charged the full, but still very reasonable cost, generally much less than at home in North America.

Gaye and I, having *discovered* a number of these spa resorts in the Czech Republic, Hungary and Germany, have experienced more than a few memorable "snapshots".

Near the mountainous western border of the Czech Republic, are a trio of world-class, pedestrian-friendly resort-like spa towns, one of which is Karlovy Vary. It is not unlike Banff, one of Canada's premier all-season playgrounds. The town boasts numerous hot springs, each of which has been tapped and piped to public drinking fountains, scattered throughout the pedestrian-only promenade.

The very hot mineral water in each spring is identified by its mineral content, medicinal properties, and the condition it treats. Believers from all over Europe flock there to "take the cure". To treat various ailments, physicians prescribe waters from one or more of these springs.

Eye-catching purpose-designed porcelain "sipping cups" are available for purchase everywhere. It is quite a sight - visitors of many nationalities strolling the promenade, sipping their mineral water through special, curved spouts built into each cup.

Not only do we glimpse patients wholeheartedly immersing themselves in the therapeutic process while "taking the cure", we have also watched in awe as many believers crowd around the fountains, filling large containers, labelling each for its specific properties, and loading them into cars for the trip home.

One really must be either a believer in the waters' healing properties, or desperate. We have sampled the waters from many of these springs. Sediment aside, we have yet to find a spring that does not taste quite dreadful! Truth be told, we would prefer a therapeutic *sip* of ice-cold *Becherovka*. Produced only in Karlovy Vary, it is a potent concoction of more than thirty herbs. Czechs imbibe it as an aperitif to prepare the digestive system before a meal.

....

On one occasion however, we saw first-hand proof that the advertised benefits of these springs really do exist!

Jack and Anita joined us in Karlovy Vary, at one of our favourite spa lodgings—Lazne III. Prior to arriving, Anita had been experiencing problems with her digestive system.

One of the mineral springs declared its effectiveness in the restoration of digestive system balance. Anita dutifully sipped from her special cup. Not minding the taste, she decided to take even more of the hot spring water back to her room. Being ever helpful, I acquired a large empty bottle and filled it for her, from the continuously running fountain.

Next morning, only Jack appeared for breakfast. He told us that the waters had worked so well, Anita could not leave their room that morning! Her problem had been successfully over-treated!

....

Flushed with success, Anita eventually reappeared, ready to continue our adventures. I suggested that she might enjoy an underwater massage, reputed to be therapeutic, soothing and relaxing. She jumped at the offer. I booked and paid for her $8 treatment, later that afternoon.

the naked traveller

At dinner that evening, we were pummeled with laughter as she regaled us with the details of her latest adventure. Wearing her bathing suit under a robe, Anita had arrived for her appointment in a spartan, but private cubicle. A substantial, non-English-speaking woman dressed in a starched white uniform, was filling a deep metal tub with hot water. Upon seeing the bathing suit, she repeatedly gestured for Anita to remove it. Finally, Anita reluctantly complied, and following instructions, climbed up over and into the very full tub of water.

Bobbing on the surface of the very warm mineralized water, Anita began to unwind. All thoughts of relaxation subsided suddenly, as the attendant picked up what appeared to be a hefty two-inch fire hose. Immersing the nozzle in the water beside Anita, she turned on its high-pressure water flow. Pushing Anita's body under the water with one massive hand, and directing the powerful hose with the other, the attendant proceeded to massage Anita, head to toe, with the powerful water-jet. Once finished one side, she flipped Anita over, and proceeded to repeat the exercise. By the time she emerged thirty minutes later, Anita had not drowned, but was totally limp - like a wet noodle!

I still remind Anita that it was the best $8 I ever spent.

....

If shyness prevents you from appearing in public in the *altogether*, many European spa pools are not for you! Europeans have a very relaxed attitude toward nudity. Some spa pools do not permit the public to wear bathing suits. Some pools *do* designate specific days of the week for exclusive male or female use. All other days are generally for mixed bathing. It is not uncommon to see whole families, both sexes of all ages, sharing the same mineral pool.

One last anecdote:

Gaye's parents once accompanied us to the Czech Republic. We travelled by train to this same spa resort. One morning at breakfast I asked them if they would like to accompany me to the baths later that day. Gaye's mom was quite interested until I added that bathing suits were not permitted.

I can still hear Gaye's father, Bill, firmly stating,"Peter, we're not into THAT sort of thing! We'll all have an afternoon nap while YOU go into the pool!"

....

Europe boasts many spectacular, architecturally-appealing spas. The most memorable, for me, was the spa in the famous Gellert Hotel in Budapest. The majestic pool reminds one of yesteryear's beautifully decorated, ancient Roman baths. Indeed royalty from all over the world is reputed to have visited this hotel, to revel in the spa experience in truly magnificent surroundings. Don't miss this one if you are in Hungary. And yes, they *will* let you wear a bathing suit!

TIP # 46...... **The European spa experience is worth trying at least once. To minimize your cost, shop for it like a local, once you arrive in the country.**

· ·

CHAPTER NINETEEN

THE CRUISE VACATION

Follow in the wake of Magellan...Cruise the clear blue waters of the Yasawa Islands...Explore the majestic fjords of Scandinavia...

The term "cruise" invokes romantic dreams of grand ocean-going passenger liners, as well as the simpler pleasures of drifting along on compact, intimate river boats and canal barges. More about the latter in the next chapter. This chapter will focus on ocean-going cruise vacations.

We took our first cruise in the winter of 1972. We were living in Fort McMurray, in northern Alberta. Temperatures rarely rose above minus 30 Celsius in January. I still remember the thrill of booking the package—a round-trip flight and two-week cruise through the Eastern Caribbean, out of Miami. We were, by 20 or 30 years, the youngest passengers on that cruise ship.

Our cost, for the two-week all-inclusive holiday, was $3,000; a very expensive luxury-trip in those days!

Travellers today are very fortunate; they are able to book similar fly-and-cruise combinations, often for less than we paid some 35 years ago!

At the high-end, luxury ships feature pampered cruising to exotic destinations such as the Galapagos or Micronesia. If you are on a tight budget, these trips will not yet be on your list.

However, do not despair. Today's cruise industry is extremely competitive.

peter dolezal

Some 24 major cruise lines compete fiercely to fill more than 160 ships in their fleets. The number, size, and amenities of new ships is increasing annually. In 2008 alone, over 22,000 beds were added in the world-wide cruising industry.

Cruise lines have become more and more creative in offering a wide variety of incentives to attract repeat customers.

With so many berths available world-wide, the smart traveller can pick up marvelous bargains. Simply by investing time in research, and exercising some flexibility on dates and destinations, you will find many bargains—some truly astounding!

If you have the flexibility, check "last-minute" offerings, within a month of when you are considering embarking on a cruise. Two excellent sites are ***www.portsandbows.com*** and ***www.vacationstogo. com***.

As the beginning or end of a region's cruise season nears, you may find particularly enticing bargains. As with air carriers, it costs very little extra to fill those last, otherwise-empty cabins. The cruise line would rather sell its last vacant cabins at a fraction of the posted price, than sail with them empty.

As an exercise in October, I googled **last minute cruises** departing over the next 30 days. The results yielded literally dozens of bargains, on 5-star ships, for seven to fourteen-day cruises. Prices started at $595 per person, plus taxes. Continuing the search, I confirmed that bargain air fares were also available, to connect passengers with these highly-discounted cruises.

On the same day that I found the above example, we received a Princess Cruises flyer in the mail, offering a 7-day Caribbean cruise in a balcony-stateroom at $799 per person, plus taxes—a real bargain.

....

Aside from " last-minute" bargains, the best cruise values are perhaps those to be found on annual *repositioning cruises.*

Every summer for example, dozens of ships navigate the waters of the west coast of North America to and from Alaska. By late September, most of these ships have begun *repositioning* to Florida ports, via the Panama Canal, in preparation for the winter's Caribbean or South American cruise season. In late April, the process is reversed, and the ships once again reposition to the West Coast for their Alaska cruise season.

As I write this, the best repositioning deal I can find is a 19-day cruise at the beginning of November, on Norwegian Cruise Lines sailing from San Francisco to Santiago, Chile. The incredible bargain-basement starting price, of $499 per person, works out to only $30 per person, per day, when all taxes and port charges are added! Even balcony-cabins are only $999, or $60 per day, with taxes. *At these prices, you might actually save money by taking the cruise, rather than staying at home!*

A traveller may covet a 14 to 20-day trans-Panama Canal cruise. During either the spring or fall repositioning period, he can find many a bargain price. It will often *include* connecting flights, with fares as much as 50% below normal posted rates. The repeat customer, loyal to a particular cruise line, will often be offered a cabin upgrade at no extra cost. *Whether such is offered or not—ask. You may be pleasantly surprised.*

A distinct advantage of cruise holidays, is that the traveller can predict, to within a few hundred dollars, the total cost of the trip. It is generally the discretionary expenses—shopping, the bar bill, and the casino, that can put a big dent in one's wallet. Major additional expenses should be little other than optional *shore excursions*, at each port of call.

Pre-booking shore excursions is advisable, either on-line directly through the cruise line, or through your booking agent, well before your departure. This will ensure that:

- The excursions in which you are particularly interested, are not sold-out, as usually happens if you wait till after boarding;
- You can more accurately predict your total holiday cost;
- You can plan your *discretionary* spending budget.

Unless you opt for the ultimate in high-end cruises, or *must* have the best accommodation on the ship, you will find the cost per-person, per-day, to be among the most economical and best-value means of enjoying a luxurious holiday, with superb service, gourmet dining and first-class entertainment included. The only unknown is your degree of willpower in limiting discretionary spending.

For the determined budget-minded, keep in mind that the less-expensive *inside* cabins, aside from the lack of view, offer all the amenities of pricier outer cabins. Considering how little time one in fact spends in the cabin, choosing an inside cabin may be a wise economic decision. It may well save you enough to pay for all your shore excursions.

Since our introduction to cruise vacations almost 40 years ago, we have enjoyed Caribbean, South American, Fijian and Alaska cruises, always in an outside cabin, for as little as $125 per person per day. Similar prices continue to be available to this day.

....

If you have the time and flexibility to take advantage of extended voyages on select freighters, check out www.freighter-cruises.com.

Some 29,000 freighters ply the world's oceans. About 300 of them offer a limited number of passenger cabins at very reasonable prices. While a freighter will not boast most of the amenities and luxuries of the big passenger liners, they often offer unique ports of call, larger cabins, gourmet meals with the captain and officers, and a very private experience, usually with, at most, a dozen passengers.

A significant perk of freighter travel: the usual layover in each port is two or three days, allowing much more time for exploration ashore, than the usual cruise ship offerings of eight or ten hours.

All in all, freighter cruises represent great value, and deserve serious consideration.

> **TIP # 47 ....** **Cruise holidays, whether on a passenger ship or freighter, can represent superb value. Book early if your schedule is inflexible. Otherwise, look for last-minute bargain offers, or repositioning cruises.**

CHAPTER TWENTY

RIVER CRUISING

"Cruising down the river, on a lazy afternoon ...". A 1953 song that never loses its appeal.

A fast-growing segment of the cruise industry is river cruising. It is particularly suited to the fascinating waterways criss-crossing Europe. Dozens of long, low-slung river-boats can be seen tied up in the *centre* of virtually every major city along Europe's rivers.

- More and more North Americans are drawn to the charms of the rivers and canals of the U.K. and continental Europe.

- Aboard a paddle-wheeler, you can explore the historic Mississippi River.

- "Pocket" ships offer a glimpse of Canada's and Russia's vastness as they cruise the waters of the St. Lawrence Seaway and the Volga River system.

- China's Yangtze, Brazil's Amazon, and Egypt's Nile are also attracting increasing numbers of river-cruising tourists.

Google **River Cruises**. Choose a destination. Within seconds, you will find yourself *afloat* in numerous options and price ranges.

River cruising is a spectacular way to travel. While not for the truly budget-conscious, it need not be any more expensive than travelling around on one's own, by rental car or train, staying in quality accommodations, and eating out for each meal. This is particularly true in the U.K. and continental Europe.

Many tour companies offer for instance, 7 to 14-day European river cruises featuring personalized service, superb almost-close-enough-to-touch scenery, and unique centuries-old ports of call. Prices range from $1,500 to $3,000 per person, per week, depending on the itinerary, the ship's amenities, and cabin size.

If we for example, choose a per-person mid-range figure of $2,250 per week, the $4,500 cost *for a couple* works out to about $640 per day. At first glance, this appears exorbitantly expensive. However, the cost seems much more reasonable, once one considers that this price typically includes, for *each person*:

- Seven days of leisurely cruising through exquisite countryside;
- Seven nights of accommodation in a well-appointed, comfortable, view cabin;
- 21 full-course gourmet meals, featuring local specialties;
- Seven days of guided walks, cycling, or bus tours;
- Miscellaneous extras, such as beverages, entry fees to attractions, and occasionally, on-board entertainment.

If you should be fortunate enough to combine your river cruise with a *free* flight, having for example, redeemed accumulated reward-mileage points, your river cruise becomes an even better value.

Consider these additional advantages of river cruising:

- As with all cruising, unpack only once, yet visit many renowned destinations;
- Casual dress - dinners are at most, casually elegant;
- Gourmet food - savour regional flavors;
- Maximum of 120 to 180 passengers - an intimate cruising experience;
- All outside cabins with large windows, and in some cases balconies - the view comes to you, even in your robe and slippers;

- Moor in the heart of Europe's historic town centres - easy access for impromptu shopping and sightseeing;
- Bicycles often available for shore excursions - light exercise while you sightsee;
- Local guides and lecturers, with expertise on regional lore, customs and historical sites, enrich the cruise experience;
- Smoke-free environment, except in limited designated outdoor areas.

....

Well-travelled friends John and Lenore bemoaned the fact that, due to John's failing eyesight, their travelling days were over. They had been all over the world, but had never experienced a river cruise. They decided to take one last trip, along the waterways of central Europe.

They booked passage with a company specializing in river cruises worldwide, a Canadian tour operator who provides a first-class door-to-door, all-inclusive service.

Two-weeks later, they returned home, bubbling over with enthusiasm and excitement, extolling the accommodation, the food, the people, and the entire experience.

Even with failing eyesight, John was able to revel in the sounds, scents and tastes of the region.

As we go to print, John and Lenore are discussing their next "one-last-trip"!

All in all, a great way to experience Europe!

....

Many river-cruise operators offer discounted airfares from North America, as well as optional travel extensions, before or after the cruise, at *better* rates than you are likely to arrange yourself.

Once is not enough! There are devotees who enjoy this mode of travel so much that they return to it exclusively, year after year. Everyone should try this type of holiday at least once.

> **TIP # 48 ..... River-cruising can be a very low-stress, reasonably-priced means of visiting many European cities, in an intimate and luxurious manner. However, it is not for the budget traveller.**

....

CHAPTER TWENTY-ONE

THE CYCLING HOLIDAY

If, like ourselves, you are an enthusiastic cyclist, you can enjoy memorable budget-wise adventures, both in North America and overseas. All one needs is a reasonable degree of fitness, a dependable bicycle, and a sense of adventure.

Google ***Cycling Holidays*** for hundreds of options and locations.

Of our many cycling adventures with friends Sandra and Dennis, one was a ten-day bicycle tour around Prince Edward Island, on Canada's east coast. Our sturdy touring bicycles survived their long flights in their cardboard cartons. In Charlottetown, we loaded the panniers, strapped on our helmets, and set off in search of lobster, mussel and Malpeque oyster feasts.

P.E.I., a dazzling province to tour by bicycle, is not unlike Ireland, with its green, rolling hills. Because there are no mountains, we were lulled into expecting an easy ride. The constant offshore breezes, while refreshing, made us feel like we were pedaling uphill most of the time! After a day of hard cycling, we were delighted to be spoiled by the royal treatment we received from our smiling, laid-back B&B hosts, who often lent us their family vehicle so we could drive ourselves to another mouth-watering seafood dinner.

....

As with other forms of travel, these vacations can span the whole price spectrum:

- Super-deluxe guided tours;

- The self-arranged bed-and-breakfast / guesthouse route;
- The ultimate in economy, the bed-on-your-back camping solution.

1. AIR - TRAVEL WITH YOUR BICYCLE

With today's ever-changing weight and luggage-size restrictions, it has become a challenge to transport full-size bicycles on a plane. Years ago, they were simply stuffed, along with panniers, into airline-supplied cartons, and checked at no extra cost, as one piece of your luggage.

Today, you are more likely to pay a hefty oversize-luggage charge, *and* have to provide your own packaging.

....

One solution is to *rent bicycles* at your destination.

We once did this in Florida. After a few painful hours we were so relieved to crawl off the ancient, cumbersome beasts with their unforgiving tractor-style seats, that we vowed "never again"!

Today's rental bicycles are, unlike our Florida experience, usually state-of-the-art. Touring cycles, for longer road trips, often come complete with panniers, and even GPS systems. Rentals can be arranged on-the-spot, but are best pre-booked well ahead of your arrival date, particularly for popular areas in high season.

....

There *are* other solutions, particularly if you plan frequent cycling holidays, and prefer your own bicycle.

Consider this, for instance. A number of North American manufacturers now offer a deluxe version of the *folding bicycle* that we have seen, for many years, as favourites of camping enthusiasts, and RV'ers.

Eugene, Oregon, boasts several companies dedicated to the manufacture of state-of-the-art, high-tech bicycles, which fold into their own custom-tailored suitcase. The case can be checked on any airline as one of your bags. Relatively lightweight, it can easily accompany you on any train, plane or bus trip. Once at your destination, you quickly hit the road with that same bicycle suitcase now efficiently attached as a mini-trailer, to the back of your bicycle!

These unique two-wheelers, eye-stopping to say the least, are lightweight and geared in such an efficient manner that they perform as well as most full-size touring units.

Bike Friday in Eugene, Oregon, is a particular favourite of many cyclists. Check their website at *www.bikefriday.com.*

Full-size, collapsible, even tandem touring bicycles are available from several other manufacturers. Google *Folding Bicycles* for more information.

Aside from their handy compact size, the custom suitcase will ensure that your bicycle arrives undamaged at your destination.

The cost of investing in these deluxe, custom-made folding bicycles is significant, starting at about $1,500 for a fully-equipped unit, plus the optional cost of the custom suitcase. If however, you are a cycling enthusiast dreaming of major trips, you may well invest a similar amount for a well-built full-size touring bicycle.

2. RAIL TRAVEL WITH YOUR BICYCLE

Whether travelling with a compact collapsible unit in a custom case, or a full-size bicycle, transport by train is relatively easy. Occasionally in North America, but more particularly in Europe where bicycles are a common mode of transportation, designated wagons on trains are equipped specifically to safely transport bicycles.

Closer to home, again with Sandra and Dennis, we rode our trusty full-size touring bicycles over the bridges of Vancouver to its train station. From there, bicycles securely tethered in the baggage wagon, we relaxed as the train carried us to Jasper, Alberta, in Canada's Rocky Mountains. We once again mounted up, our panniers stuffed to over-flowing. We huffed and puffed our way along the spectacular, but mountainous Icefields route to Banff. At the end of each day we revelled in the luxury of well-earned long, hot soaks at each of four lodges we had pre-booked along the route.

A mountain-side chalet in Canmore, Alberta, site of many 1988 Winter Olympic events, became our temporary home base. From there we explored the at-times demanding natural beauty of the Lake Louise and Kananaskis areas. With great reluctance at week's end, our valiant "steeds" once again in the baggage car, we climbed aboard the train in Banff, homeward-bound.

Travelling by train meant that we:

- Left our vehicles at home;
- Lessened our carbon footprint significantly;
- Enjoyed a quick, comfortable, and stress-free journey to and from our cycling destination.

A more economical option, had we chosen it, would have been to *camp* in the exquisite natural beauty of the mountains. Camping would have stretched our budget significantly.

For us, however, the objective was to work hard all day, to be pampered by hot water, a delicious meal, and a cozy bed, at the end of each day.

3. BUS TRAVEL WITH YOUR BICYCLE

Although some long-distance bus lines are now equipped to carry a few full-size bicycles, most are not. Again, with this economical mode of transportation, the collapsible-bicycle-in-a-suitcase would allow you the greater flexibility, during your planned cycling tour.

This option is particularly suited to travel in Europe, where long-distance bus passes are very affordable, compared to the generally, more expensive train and plane travel.

4. THE ALL - INCLUSIVE ORGANIZED TOUR

Recreational cycling is a world-wide passion. Tours are offered in North America, the U.K., continental Europe, Australia, New Zealand, and Asia. If you google *Bicycling Tours* for any given destination, you'll find enough options, from the very basic back-to-nature, to the ultra-luxurious, to last you a lifetime of cycling adventures.

As to be expected, the more exotic the destination, the higher the price. The package you select *may* include airfare; in most cases however, you must arrange your own flights.

In some countries, such as Vietnam and China, traffic concerns and/or travel restrictions make it advisable and even mandatory, for one's safety, to travel in an organized group.

The great advantage of *organized tours*, regardless of price or amenities, is that all of the planning is done for you. Accommodations and meals are arranged at logical distances. More appealing however, is that, other than your day-pack, all luggage is usually transported for you from one nightly stop to the next. No heavy panniers to weigh you down.

Although most tours will supply a reliable bicycle, experienced cyclists often prefer the comfort and known quirks of their own. When a bicycle is supplied, do your homework! Verify that you will be happy with its quality. Determine as well, whether you must supply your own helmet; helmet-use is still rare in some countries.

....

In North America, cycling tours can be found at prices starting at about $600 per week for a low-budget camping tour. At the upper end are the very expensive all-inclusive options which include deluxe dining and accommodations, as well as extras such as wine tastings, spa treatments, or other themes around which your guide might build a unique tour.

Some tour operators offer a combination of "roughing it" and deluxe. They do the cooking. They carry the gear. They set up the tents, usually in awesome settings which on your own, you may never have discovered.

Marathon coast-to-coast tours of 60 to 70 days are steadily gaining momentum across both Canada and the United States. They start at about $6,000 for the camping version.

We have encountered many such tour groups participating in a west-to-east, wind-at-their-back adventure across Canada. More than a few of these riders are fit senior citizens, well into their 70's! Both humbling and inspiring, they never cease to amaze us.

....

All-inclusive cycling tours are generally *not* for the bargain-hunter. Plenty of opportunities exist however, for budget-wise group cycling/camping adventures, with riders taking turns at cooking duties. Obviously, the latter would be far more affordable than the luxury version with its en-route gourmet picnics, and pampered attention in comfortable lodgings at day's end.

Before committing to a specific tour, survey the options for your intended destination. Depending on the combination of itinerary, quality of accommodation and included features, you will find a wide spectrum of prices. If you want to stay every night in deluxe chalets in Switzerland, choose that option. Be prepared however, to pay for the privilege.

....

European Canal or River Cruises often go hand-in-hand with bicycles. You can work off your lunch with a leisurely "rocking-chair" ride along the riverbank. More energetically, the enthusiast can ride ahead each day, while still enjoying great accommodation and meals on board. The tour operator will often make bicycles available, while some riders bring their own, perhaps planning additional cycling excursions. Again, the collapsible bike would be a perfect option.

5. THE DELUXE ROUTE ON THE CHEAP!

Thanks to the internet, it is a simple task to independently determine the most interesting, appealing and scenic routes in your destination-of-choice.

You have at your fingertips, on the websites of any number of cycle-tour companies, itineraries, maps, and schedules, designed to attract potential clients. Use these sites as a primary resource.

The tour companies have done much of the homework for you. From much experience with scores of cyclists, from novice to expert, they have refined their offerings. For you, this is a heaven-sent opportunity to simply and efficiently *borrow* the best routes, calculate daily distances, and perhaps even research locations for over-night stops.

At no cost to you, you can benefit from that expertise. Simply refine the specifics to your own schedule, itinerary and budget.

Once you have determined your destination and planned a route, you can then decide how much of your travel budget you wish to spend, for various levels of comfort and amenities:

- Rent a bicycle or bring your own?
- Camping? Hostelling? B&B? Other?

You can save a little or a lot, depending on the touring style you choose.

Remember however, that with an independently-planned tour, the one key service you will usually have to forego, is the transport of your luggage between nightly stops. This option then, is *not* for those who really cannot travel light, nor refrain from acquiring enroute, bulky souvenirs.

We did in fact, once buy a case of wine while on a cycling holiday. Luckily, the winery was not far from our home, at an early stop on our tour. The following week we were able to retrace our route by car, enjoy a lunch at the winery, and collect our now two, cases of wine.

On yet another cycling adventure we became so enamored of a hand-crafted, cedar garden bench, that we blew our travel budget and bought it, but only after the vendor agreed to deliver it to our home on his next trip to our community.

....

With our cycling companions, we have adapted smart-trip options from books, magazines, and the web, for many locales in North America. We usually opt for B&B accommodations along the way, enjoying the opportunity to mix and chat with other travellers who often provide tips on local things to see or do, places to eat, and even where to stay next. We have cycled many thousands of kilometers over the years, always making our own arrangements, and having through experience, learned to travel light!

The bonus was that our cost was always half, or even less, than we would have paid for a supported tour. This allowed us to splurge on evenings of well-deserved wining and dining!

6. THE HYBRID TOUR

It is becoming easier to enjoy the advantages of both worlds, combining some of the benefits and conveniences of an organized, guided tour, with the economy and freedom of independent travel.

Other friends, seasoned cyclists who have ventured far and wide, recently returned from an eight-day cycling trip between Vienna, Austria, and Cesky Krumlov, in the Czech Republic. A local tour company provided the sturdy bicycles, a route map, a portable GPS, and a cell phone, along with detailed directions to pre-arranged accommodation each night. Each day the tour operator picked up and delivered the luggage from the previous night's hotel or guesthouse to the next. With lightweight daypacks only, and no predetermined daily itinerary, our friends rode on their own, greatly enjoying the flexibility of departing, arriving, stopping, and making interesting detours, as they wished.

They found this to be such an economical alternative to the fully-supported trip they had originally considered joining, that no sooner were they home, than they were researching their next destination and route.

Similar tour arrangements are available throughout most countries in Europe. For a start, two useful European websites offering these options are ***www.topbicycle.com*** and ***www.discoverfrance.com***.

....

7. CYCLING "SNAPSHOTS"

A cycling vacation provides daily exercise, maintains fitness, and even permits hearty dining-without-guilt, all while immersing oneself in other cultures and unique settings.

Recognize however, that this is *not* a fully-pampered holiday! There is a certain element of roughing it. You will *not* find a porta-potty whenever you need one. Your bicycle will not always cooperate. It will at some point, have a flat tire or mechanical problem. The weather will not always be ideal. You will encounter sweltering heat, rain, and wind. But without a doubt, you *will* have memorable experiences that

the naked traveller

will bring back a smile for years to come.

Let me share with you, a couple of our cycling *snapshots*:

With our friends, we arrived at our reserved B&B, in a seaside town in Washington state. Feeling charitable that day, I suggested that the others go in, register, and clean up, while I put away the bicycles and lock them up for the night.

By the time I entered, my wife and friends were ensconced in the parlour, enjoying hot tea and scones. I decided to shower before joining them. Gaye directed me to our room at the end of the hall on the second floor.

Up I went, turned at the top of the staircase, and continued to the door at the end of the hall. Since there were no locks, I simply opened the door and stepped into the room.

*My wife and friends downstairs heard my shocked exclamation— "What the *?!..."!*

I had walked in on a couple, intimately engaged, in the middle of what I thought was my bed! I quickly mumbled an apology. "That's OK!", the woman calmly replied as I stumbled out, somehow having the presence of mind to close the door behind me.

After locating "our" room at the opposite end of the hall, I finally had my shower.

You can well imagine my surprise and awkwardness fifteen minutes later, when I joined the tea party downstairs to see Gaye and our friends, comfortably chatting with the couple whom I had so indelicately disturbed. They seemingly, were not at all embarrassed!

....

After a long day on our bicycles, at yet another B&B, we were deeply asleep in one of three rooms which shared a common bathroom.

Our friends were in the second room, and a single traveller, in the third.

Suddenly we were awakened by the opening of our door, and someone walking into our room. Apparently needing the bathroom, the lone gentleman was either sleepwalking, or disoriented, as he headed straight for the antique wash bowl on the low dresser.

Gaye, always the diplomat, in her best teacher's voice, softly coached, "Turn around, go out the door, turn right, go down the hall to the bathroom on your right". Sure enough, the man, now in obvious dire straits, turned and did exactly as told, hopefully to reach his objective in time!

The next morning, at our communal breakfast table set for five, the gentleman gobbled his food, said not a word, and made a hasty departure.

Cycling is always an adventure. We will *all* encounter interesting, unique and colourful situations while cycling, especially when staying at B&B's or campgrounds, where the environment is communal.

TIP # 49 ..... For those so inclined, memorable cycling holidays are available world-wide, with varying levels of support, and at great variations in cost. Using the internet as your best friend, choose the option that best meets your budget and needs.

CHAPTER TWENTY-TWO

THE HIKING HOLIDAY

Adventure awaits around every bend in the trail, for all who enjoy the challenge of hiking and trekking holidays. There are very few places in the world unavailable to those on foot.

As trekking throughout the globe gains in popularity, North America, the U.K., and continental Europe continue to be favoured destinations. China, Tibet, Argentina and Chile are steadily gaining ground as new frontiers for hikers. This type of holiday appeals to many: the young and the young-at-heart; the solitary loner and small groups; urbanites and mountaineers. Google *Hiking Holidays* and pick your route.

In Manning Provincial Park in southern British Columbia, we met a young man who, solo, had just completed a four-month trek along the Pacific Crest Trail, from its southern terminus at the Mexico-U.S. border. He did not appear to have an ounce of fat on his body, had a long, straggly beard, and craved only a huge salad for dinner!

A hiking holiday can range from self-organized, to a fully-escorted tour, with the price-range covering the whole spectrum, from low-budget to ultra-expensive.

As with bicycle touring, it is easy to *adopt* routes and itineraries meticulously researched, planned, and organized by professional tour groups. Use them as guidelines for your own, *budget-wise* trek, as you make arrangements for meals and accommodation.

The biggest issue, as always, is luggage. Most of us, certainly once we reach a certain age, no longer wish to carry a 40-pound pack on our back as we wander the world on foot.

Is there an inexpensive solution? My wife and I have arrived at, for us, a very workable alternative, which we have repeatedly put into practice.

As mentioned earlier, Canadian provincial Automobile Associations offer a growing inventory of long-stay holidays, with four-week minimum stays, in an expanding number of countries, such as Portugal, Spain, France, Hawaii, Mexico, and New Zealand. New locales are added yearly. Rates generally start at a very reasonable $1,200 per person, with full kitchen facilities included. Air fare is an optional add-on.

One winter we spent an active, but easy five weeks, on the French Riviera. Our home-away-from-home was an apartment in Menton, near the Italian border. Every day, carrying only small daypacks, we hiked further and further westward, along the Riviera's coastline.

Even with occasional days off for laundry or just time-out, we trekked over 500 kilometers during our five weeks, exploring all the famous seaside towns including Monaco, Nice, Villefranche, Cap-d'Ail, Antibes, Cannes and St. Raphael.

Each day, after fresh, warm croissants for breakfast in our small but comfortable apartment, we set out, often stopping in early afternoon for our one big meal of the day. In late afternoon we hopped aboard one of the frequent local trains, back home to Menton.

The next morning, the train took us back to where we had left off the previous day. We carried on hiking, not knowing what treasure awaited us—a Picasso Museum? A Rothschild chateau? A lively village market?

On the spur of the moment, we would often decide to divert up the incredibly-steep hillside paths above the Mediterranean, to find ourselves in another world - ancient, sleepy villages perched on the cliffs overlooking the sparkling sea.

At midday, on a bench by the sea, or on a hillside under flowering almond trees, we often enjoyed an alfresco picnic of local delicacies. On other occasions, we stopped instead at a small local bistro, where we ordered the daily lunch special, the "plat du jour". This dish, much less expensive than ordering "a la carte" from the menu, was usually more than enough food to carry us through the rest of the day, and introduced us to many favourite local dishes. If we were particularly hungry, we ordered instead, the "Table d'Hote", a reasonably-priced, three or four-course meal.

In the evening, with well-worn shoes removed, and the scent of thousands of ripening lemon trees wafting through the window, a freshly-baked baguette, delectable cheeses, slices of pear, rich fig jam, and a bottle of good local wine, were all we needed. What could be more magical, or more economical?

Despite fairly pricey train costs, these five weeks turned out to be one of our most economical holidays. Here we were in February, in mostly sunny, perfect hiking weather of 12 to 14 degrees Celsius, on the world-famous Riviera, at not much greater cost than had we stayed home.

Had we visited during the prime summer tourist season, our apartment would have cost at minimum, $240 per day, instead of our off-season bargain - about $50 per day.

Keeping in mind that five pounds can feel like ten by the end of a long day of hiking, we always attempt to travel light. But there are some items—a waterproof windbreaker, water bottle, sunscreen, map and camera, which we simply must have. In this case, we were glad to have not only our pedometer which challenged us to greater distances, but also our collapsible hiking poles for those steep hillsides.

....

Several winters later, we enjoyed a similar, long-stay vacation in southern Portugal's Algarve region. Again, over a six-week period we hiked hundreds of kilometers along the Atlantic coast, with midday breaks in seaside fishing villages to devour meals of grilled freshly-caught seafood.

The only difference this time was that local trains were not convenient for daily travel back and forth from our hikes. Instead, we jumped on local buses which proved in fact much cheaper than trains, and which, as they wove their way along, provided us with a glimpse of other villages, and countryside through which we had not trekked.

Despite the addition of excursions to Lisbon, Seville, Gibraltar, and Tangier, where we continued our explorations on foot, this low-key walking holiday was again very economical. In total, it cost even less than our previous sojourn on the French Riviera.

*An added bonus: We found southern Portugal to be four or five degrees warmer than were the same winter months in France. Only to say that I had done it, did I jump into the Atlantic a few times. My swims however, were **not** memorable for their duration!*

Tip # 50 …. Always keep a copy of local bus and/or train timetables in your daypack. Being stranded overnight because you missed the last train or bus, can really blow your budget on a long taxi ride or last-minute overnight accommodation.

Long-stay hiking holidays of this nature are easily organized virtually world-wide, even when travel retailers do not offer a "package" for your chosen destination. Another example:

One winter we independently arranged a five-week sojourn in Sydney, Australia. With substantial effort, we researched holiday apartment rentals on the web. We then relied on Val, a trusted Sydney friend, to check out first-hand, our various options on the Manly waterfront. We settled on a charming one-bedroom apartment, directly across from the beach.

We flew Business Class, using our travel reward-miles. To break up the long flight, our tickets allowed us an enroute stop-over of several days in Honolulu, Hawaii.

Once settled into our new "down-under" home, we again began to explore on foot. Hiking was not always easy in Australia's extreme summer heat and humidity. Our daypacks were heavier than usual with extra water, but the thought of discontinuing our daily treks never occurred to us. Our explorations covered some 120 kilometers of the Sydney Harbour shoreline and environs. We visited countless unique, often colourful neighbourhoods, the Taronga Zoo, Sydney Harbour Bridge, and Darling Harbour. Never ready to call it quits, our wanderings continued both north and south along the coast, to famous beaches such as Bondi.

Some of our daily treks had us scrambling along bush trails where we saw and heard kookaburras, cockatoos, lorikeets, and once, not entirely enthusiastically, a large sinuous snake. Happily the snake was even less charmed by us and disappeared in a flash!

For transportation in the Sydney area, we used local buses and harbour ferries to get us to and from our hiking points. At the end of five weeks, our trusty pedometer read 480 kilometers!

Despite a number of side excursions to the Blue Mountains and various wildlife sanctuaries, our walking holiday was again very reasonably priced, particularly given our budget-stretching free air fare! This included too, acknowledging Val's contribution to our budget-wise holiday, by inviting her and brother Robert, to be our guests at their favourite local eateries.

TIP # 51….. Enlist friends or acquaintances at your destination as a key, knowledgeable, local resource in helping you achieve best-value. They know the local bargains in accommodations, and the most worthwhile excursions.

……………………………..

We have enjoyed shorter versions of similar budget-wise walking vacations in the Czech Republic, the Austrian and Swiss countrysides, and the Cinqueterre on the Italian Riviera. Even exploration on foot, of large cities such as San Francisco, Hong Kong, Buenos Aires, Prague, London, Paris, and Rome has given us reasonably economical holidays.

Although many walkers/hikers opt for multi-day point-to-point treks, from one location to another, we have preferred hiking from a *home-base* to which we return each evening. The hassle of packing, unpacking, and hauling heavy backpacks is avoided.

What is best for us however, is that we become temporary, and at times even recognized, residents of the town or region that is the current focus of each of our hiking holidays.

Once, on the hills above Monte Carlo, we encountered a spry 80-something couple who, while we laboured beside them, conquered the hills like young billy goats. When we bumped into the couple again a few days later, they greeted us like old friends - introducing us to their acquaintances as "our Canadian friends who came here to hike—can you imagine that!"

We have always chosen to explore independently, with a tentative plan for the day, but without a structured itinerary. Tours however, to all of these destinations could have been arranged, in detail, with few surprises, through professional tour companies. Costs would definitely have been considerably higher.

Perhaps more important for us, we would have missed out on the gratification and anticipation of doing our own research and planning, creating and sticking to our own budget.

Experiencing the inevitable, unexpected surprises which always accompany a less-structured trip is, for us, the bonus.

TIP # 52 ..... **Hiking holidays are a superb way to explore, get exercise, and appreciate local geography, cultures and peoples. If carefully planned and executed, they can also result in extremely good value for the travel dollar.**

CHAPTER TWENTY-THREE

THE CAMPING / RV HOLIDAY

- *The sight of an elk grazing nearby;*
- *The splash of a trout;*
- *The smell of the campfire at dusk;*
- *The aroma of bacon cooking in the morning air;*
- *Going for days without having to take a bath.*

If you have children or grandchildren, treat them to an unforgettable experience—camping in the great outdoors. They will love being active in this new environment, delighting in new adventures away from the conveniences of everyday life-at-home.

1. TENTING

One of the least expensive family holidays we can safely enjoy, throughout North America, Europe, Australia and New Zealand, is the camping holiday—if, in some countries you consider driving on the *wrong* side of the road to be safe!

One of my fondest early-childhood memories is of our family tenting on a month-long journey through the southern Australian states of New South Wales, Victoria and South Australia. Our vehicle was a hard-to-miss, fire-engine-red, 1953 Morris Minor convertible.

I remember still, the herds of kangaroos bouncing around near our campsite in the bush, the spectacular sight of thousands of multi-

coloured lorikeets and majestic cockatoos, and the distinctive sound of the kookaburras in the trees.

You too will benefit, saving significantly, compared to the cost of other holiday options. You need not invest heavily—a basic tent, tarp, lantern, mats and good sleeping bags. Most of your needs can be met by combing through your basement or attic, visiting a few garage sales, or borrowing from friends and family.

North America has spectacular scenery and many unique campgrounds. Pitching a tent can cost as little as $15 per night in a secure environment. The National Parks in both the U.S. and Canada offer great variety, cleanliness, and a wide range of amenities, combined with affordable fees.

2. TENT-TRAILER, TRAVEL TRAILER, OR FIFTH WHEEL

The slightly more affluent, or those who simply prefer to enjoy more pampered accommodation, while still technically "camping", can graduate from tent, to *tent-trailer, travel trailer, or fifth-wheel*, at progressively greater cost.

The greatest advantage of each of these detachable units, over the larger motor-home, is that after setting up camp, you still have access to a vehicle, for mobility.

None of our family recalls, other than from photos, the miniscule antique tent-trailer we owned when they were toddlers. The whole unit was the size of a cozy double bed. The canvas tent popped straight up above the bed, with a small extension to the ground on one side only. Amenities consisted of a zippered door and a canvas floor. Yet we enjoyed many weekend excursions, as well as a two-week adventure circling Lake Superior in this primitive unit, as much as we did years later, when we repeated the journey in a much larger, Class C motor-home, with almost all the amenities of home.

The innovation in these units, over the years, has been so phenomenal that now, a tent trailer can often sleep six or eight people. It can be soft-sided, hard-topped, and have a hydraulic set-up, as we approach the top-of-the-line units. Options include full kitchens, showers, toilets, and more storage than in some small apartments.

One can spend from $5,000 to $25,000 for these units.

Considering a purchase? Rent the first few times you use one. Travel with all the family, to confirm that this lifestyle is for you and that a purchase makes sense. You may be convinced after a week or two of use, that you would indeed use it often enough to justify the investment.

In that case, thoroughly research your options:

- What are the additional outfitting costs, such as a hitch and necessary wiring?
- What about additional insurance costs?
- Where will you store the unit ?
- Can your vehicle handle the towing weight?
- Can you afford the total cost?

Satisfied with the answers? Ready to go for it? Whoa! Stop a moment before charging ahead with a fresh-off-the-assembly-line purchase.

Consider this: Showroom-condition, low-mileage, like-new units can often be found on the ***private-resale market***. Take advantage of deals offered by those who impulsively bought first and tried a few excursions, only to decide that trailering was not their cup of tea. Often available too, are older very well-maintained units, offered for sale as couples decide either to retire from life-on-the-road, or to upgrade their unit.

If a trailer or fifth-wheel unit *is* your preferred choice, but you don't plan to travel great distances, consider renting or buying a unit in an established vacation setting, on a personal lot or "pad". Use it as your getaway cottage. Always set-up and waiting for you, this is true armchair-camping. Your new vacation *home* may come with a satellite dish, swimming pool, tennis courts, laundry facilities—perhaps even newspaper delivery!

3. THE ULTIMATE CAMPER—THE MOTOR-HOME OR "RV"

In North America we tend to refer to these larger motor-homes as *recreational vehicles*, or RV's. Don't expect however that the term will automatically be understood world-wide.

A family from Germany, exploring British Columbia in a rental RV, stopped at a Visitor Information Centre to inquire, in fluent English, about local campgrounds. When the gentleman was asked how long his RV was, he paused for a moment, then replying that he did not have one, asked if it was a requirement in Canada. The confusion was soon cleared up when he learned that his motor-home was an "RV".

Climbing up the luxury-camping ladder, one can choose to travel and "camp" in any fashion that suits both life-style and budget. Choices range from:

- The smaller Class "B" van-conversion which barely accommodates two; to
- The over-cab, Class "C" unit, which can easily sleep six; to
- The 20 to 40-foot, bus-style, Class "A".

These units can and do, serve as homes-on-wheels, not only for occasional holiday jaunts, but also for long-stay wintering in sunny climes. In late fall, in both North America and Europe, great herds of RV's hit the road, noses pointed south, only to reverse their direction, homeward-bound some months later.

To become the proud owner of one of these units, one can easily invest from $50,000 to well upwards of several hundred thousand dollars.

If you are financially comfortable, and itching to hit the road in high-style, go for it. Don't worry about how good an investment it is. You are investing in a lifestyle.

For most of us however, this kind of investment is *not* to be taken lightly. It requires research, planning, saving, and much forethought.

- Will the days of use justify the investment?
- Will financing be required?
- Is renting-out the unit feasible or desirable?
- Are the high operating and maintenance costs acceptable?
- And finally, do *all* in the family want this lifestyle?

TIP # 53 ..... Rent *before* you decide to buy a recreational vehicle; for best value, consider purchasing on the resale market.

We have, over the years, owned several motor homes. In perfect hindsight, we would have been wise, before buying, to follow this advice.

Our family thoroughly enjoyed our vacations for the two or three weeks a year that we managed to use our RV. For the rest of the year it sat, lonely and neglected, depreciating in the driveway! We could have saved many thousands of dollars had we instead rented similar units for those two or three weeks annually.

Here is a recent advertisement, pulled from the internet by googling ***Motor Home Rentals British Columbia:***

"38-foot Fleetwood Bounder, with all options, available $180/day, $1,080/week, $4,000/month, plus 32 cents per mile in excess of 100/ day."

Considering that this unit can easily represent a capital investment of $100,000, these rental rates are quite reasonable for a lengthy test-run *before* deciding to buy a similar unit.

It could be argued in fact, that unless you plan to use such a unit *very frequently*, it might be more economical to rent each year, rather than to purchase.

TIP # 54 ..... Unless you are addicted to travel with your own roof over your head, or are a "snowbird", using your expensive home-on-wheels for extended long-stays, buying a motor-home can rarely be justified on a purely-economic basis.

Needless to say, as is the case with many of our "toys", the pleasure of ownership often trumps economic logic. We should however, at least be aware of the economic realities before jumping into such a major expenditure.

TIP # 55 ..... A good rule of thumb: If you must borrow the funds to buy a recreational vehicle, you are probably wiser, economically, to rent.

Other than the high capital cost, a major disadvantage of a larger motor-home is that once you set it up, you cannot easily drive off to explore the new locale. That is, unless you invest even further, to purchase a vehicle to tow behind the unit!

A most impressive advantage of these units is that, with their bump-outs, generators, full kitchens, bathrooms, and satellite dishes, they are truly self-contained, often more modern and well-equipped than many homes.

You can often pull over on a whim and "camp" for free! In fact, some North American malls welcome overnight motor-home parking, since it enhances their night-time security, and draws you into their stores during open hours.

We have frugal friends who, for three months, travelled across Canada, with their fifth-wheel unit. They proudly reported that not once did they pay for overnight camping!

....

As always, there are exceptions to every rule, even those of economics. Here is one such:

A couple from Toronto, both retired teachers, have made their significant investment in a motor-home pay off in a rather unique manner.

When they retired, they sold their home for over $500,000. They bought a 38-foot motor-home for about $240,000. For that price, they acquired a superb unit, outfitted with every imaginable convenience. Indeed, it was meant to be their new home-on-wheels. After adding a new compact-car to be towed behind, they were now fully self-sufficient and mobile. They set off zigzagging across North America, intent on exploring as much of the continent as they could, over the next five years.

They have since wandered several hundred thousand miles, often staying for a number of months in one location, and returning for strategically-chosen visits, with children and grandchildren.

Even after investing in this deluxe unit, they were able to add almost $250,000 to their investment portfolio, the income from which acts to supplement their pensions.

Five years have now passed. The last we heard, they had no intention, for many years to come, of abandoning their vagabond RV lifestyle.

Granted, their choice is not for all. Many of us would shake our graying and balding heads, wondering how they could do such a thing— No fixed address? No weekly family gatherings? No mail?

With advances in technology leaping ahead, connection to the rest of the world is almost a non-issue. You can enjoy newscasts from your former hometown, on your laptop or your satellite TV. You can chat face-to-face with friends, children and grandchildren on your mobile phone or computer daily, as you wish.

For this particular couple, the motor-home investment was exceptionally worthwhile. They truly invested in a *lifestyle*.

....

In most cases however, recognize that you can rent quality hotel rooms and holiday accommodation, many times over, with the income from the funds that you did *not* tie up in one of these units!

TIP # 56 ..... **Owning a motor-home will allow you to travel and *camp* in style. It will probably give you great pleasure, and *may* be an excellent decision in your particular circumstance. Recognize however, that saving money through ownership, will rarely be the justification.**

. . . .

CHAPTER TWENTY-FOUR

ADVENTURE TRAVEL

Opportunities for participation in an ever-increasing variety of unique adventure and eco-tours, from moderate to extreme in their challenges, is limited only by your imagination, and your budget.

Be bold! Try something you have never before attempted in your travels. Boundaries exist only in the mind. Google *Adventure Travel* for numerous ideas and options.

On every continent you will find unique adventures, including:

- Polar expeditions,
- Heli-skiing,
- Hot-air ballooning,
- Scuba diving,
- Kayaking,
- White-water rafting,
- Mountain climbing,
- Spelunking,
- Archeological digs,
- Fishing, and
- Safari adventures.

If you want to try a bargain adventure that does not revolve around basking lazily on a beach, check out, for starters, sites such as

the naked traveller

www.intrepidtravel.com. This company, a relative newcomer, offers small group holidays at bargain prices, in many exotic areas of the world.

....

My family and I, moderately adventurous, have experienced some of the more sedate on the list:

- *In their teens, our children enthusiastically hiked, more than once, the physically demanding 75-km length of Western Canada's very rugged West Coast Trail.*

- *My wife and children, having a greater love of roughing-it than I, have several times abandoned me, for outdoor summer adventures. They have undertaken very challenging seven-day canoeing and portaging adventures, one year conquering the Nitinat Lakes area; another, the Bowron Lakes chain, both in British Columbia. They always returned home raving about the thrills of their adventures: sleeping with cans of bear-spray in hand; hanging all food-stuffs and gear high in tree branch caches; repairing a canoe leak in the middle of a lake with frantically-chewed gum; portages; rapids; downpours and clothing that would not dry.*

Now you know why I stayed behind! But if you enjoy challenging yourself both physically and mentally, in a natural environment, then rarely can you find a less expensive, yet memorable and adventurous holiday.

....

On several occasions during my corporate career, I invited major foreign clients to join me on fishing expeditions in spectacular Hakai Pass, along British Columbia's northern coastline. We flew in by float plane, to stay aboard a luxuriously outfitted floating lodge, permanently moored in a protected bay. A knowledgeable local guide escorted us, for many hours daily, on salmon-fishing marathons.

peter dolezal

If you enjoy fishing, you will appreciate the thrill of not only hooking a 6 or 8-pound Coho salmon on a six-ounce fly rod, but also managing to land it!

On one memorable occasion I had fished all day with a client from Denmark. Despite yeoman efforts by the guide, we could not entice a single bite of salmon. Not wanting to disappoint my guest, I asked the guide to take us to deeper waters to bottom-fish for halibut. Out we went, for about 30 minutes at high speed. We began to fish with heavy steel lines.

Within minutes, my guest had hooked into something very substantial. We began to think that it must be a submerged tree. But a fish it was—and what a fish! After much strenuous effort, the mammoth creature was finally hauled to the surface, where it became instantly clear that it was either we in the boat, or the fish!

Darkness quickly descended. Now severely impaired in our speed, we began laboriously chugging back to the lodge, dragging our prize.

Unbeknownst to us, our hosts had become so worried at our continued absence that they had several boats out looking for us.

We arrived safely and managed, collectively, to hoist the huge halibut onto the weigh scale. It topped 180 pounds. You can easily imagine the thrill my client experienced when he flew home a few days later, accompanied by 80 pounds of halibut fillets packed in dry ice in a custom shipping container.

He was even more thrilled some weeks later, when a photograph proudly displaying my client with his catch, was featured on the front page of the Lifestyle Section of the Toronto Globe and Mail newspaper.

The lodge operator had apparently sent the photo to the newspaper after learning that, at the time, this was the largest halibut ever landed by a sport fisherman in British Columbia. I'm sure that the framed page which I subsequently couriered to my client, still hangs proudly on a wall in Denmark!

A fishing trip of this caliber is **not** for the budget-conscious. With the cost of the charter seaplane, two or three days of luxury accommodation, gourmet food and extensive fishing, such an excursion can run into several thousand dollars per person.

But, if you want the fishing experience of a lifetime, google **Deep Sea Fishing British Columbia.** You will find many options from which to choose. Some are significantly less expensive than *my* fishing-trip-of-a-lifetime.

1. THE VOLUNTEERING VACATION

More than ever today, globetrotters are combining travel with philanthropy, embarking on ***working holidays*** in developing countries. Some spend weeks and even months on projects such as the construction of schools, hospitals and community centres. Others provide consultation on agriculture and community infrastructure programs, deliver medical care, or teach, all for no compensation.

By their very nature, these working holidays are very budget-efficient. Very basic, at times primitive, room and board is usually provided by the host community.

Your greatest cost is usually the price of your air ticket. It is only supplemental holiday travel extensions after the project finishes, for which you must budget extra dollars.

One summer, my wife, with nine other volunteer teachers, flew to Shanghai at her own expense. They were driven six hours south to Ningbo, where they were accommodated in a basic, but comfortable local hotel. They set to work on their assignment - teaching English for a month, to 250 young Chinese students. Aside from short excursions with the student body, and a day in Shanghai on their return trip, this was not even remotely, a holiday. It consisted of six-days-a-week of intense preparation, teaching, and meetings, with very little personal time.

Despite the $2,000 airfare, the extremely hot and humid climate, and the long days of hard work, my wife and her colleagues were thrilled with their experience - total immersion in another culture. The Chinese sponsors and students were equally delighted with the generosity of ten giving Canadians, several of whom were able to repeat the experience the following year.

....

Other friends participate annually in extensive and varied volunteer "building" projects in developing countries. They have laboured in Central America, South America and Africa, often accompanied by a close-knit core group of other volunteers. Living conditions, although sometimes primitive, are always safe.

The projects never seem to end. Once home, they are always delighted to share their experiences with school groups, service clubs, and church congregations, while raising funds for supplies for the next adventure. Before each mission, they collect huge quantities of clothing, medical, and school supplies to donate to the next community and its residents.

If you have the time, and wish to experience a truly unselfish "holiday" that can be of great value to less-advantaged peoples, consider such an undertaking.

For more information on such opportunities, google **Volunteer Travel**. You may find a project that is both affordable, and appealing. Such trips can be richly rewarding and satisfying experiences.

2. ECO-TOURISM

Only if you have resigned from the human race, could you be unaware of today's concern for man's impact on the environment.

Today, more and more travellers, while wishing to continue their adventures, want to do so in a manner that minimizes their resulting environmental footprint.

Such travellers now travel "green" to many locations around the world. They select holidays that focus on self-powered activities such as hiking, cycling and paddling. They fly in the latest aircraft, which produce far fewer emissions per passenger-mile than is possible even with an economy automobile. And, if they wish to truly "walk the talk", they contribute to many of the available carbon-offset programs.

Eco-tourism is becoming increasingly important. Many tour operators are adapting their offerings, aware of the need to become involved in this sector, or risk losing clients.

....

A note of caution when researching travel through those who market themselves as "eco-operators". Before booking, ask:

- Do they have a written environmental code of practice which they follow?
- Do they hire local guides who know how to minimize their "footprint"?
- Do they use the latest techniques in dealing with garbage, recycling, and wastewater?
- In short, are they *in fact* eco-practitioners, or are they simply appearing to jump on board through appealing advertising, but little real action?

A helpful starting point in your search for reputable tour operators in this sector of the industry is ***www.ecotourism.com***. An additional excellent site is ***www.wholetravel.com***. This latter site uses a rating system to rank tour operators, hotels, and resorts according to environmental practices, social and cultural support for the local community, and the effectiveness of their customer education efforts.

peter dolezal

....

If you truly are serious about minimizing *your* impact on the environment, do your part even before you leave home.

Turn off the power to your computer, printer, TV, DVD player, and at the least, all small appliances. Set your hot water tank on "vacation" mode, and turn your heating system off, or at least down to its minimum safe level. Don't leave lights on. Use light-timers instead.

TIP # 57..... **We owe it to the environment to appreciate and protect what we have. Do your part to leave nature's beauty behind for future generations to enjoy.**

CHAPTER TWENTY-FIVE

CULTURE SHOCK

Spiky purple hair....exotic multi-hued robes....unusual new food sensations...incomprehensible languages....

We need not travel far from home to experience culture shock.

A first visit to a buzzing, vibrant metropolitan city, from your small quiet rural town, can be a huge adjustment. Even within your own city, visiting an ethnic neighbourhood where English is a second language, can create culture shock.

If you travel extensively, you will undoubtedly encounter various degrees of culture shock, often eye-opening and exciting, at times very upsetting.

Don't let that deter you from travelling. Revel in it. We often surprise ourselves with our ability to adapt and learn. It's all part of the travel experience. It serves to tune us in, not only to the world as we know it, but also to the varied, colourful, and often sad world of our fellow human beings.

Coming home will take on greater significance and foster greater appreciation, the more one travels.

I will never forget the "favellas" clinging to the edge of steep muddy cliffs above Caracas, Venezuela, or those perched high on the mountainsides abutting the affluent Copacabana and Ipanema Beach areas of Rio de Janeiro, Brazil. Equally etched in my memory are the living conditions of the more-than-a-million people living in the massive Townships outside South Africa's Capetown. We were at that time, by special arrangement only, able to visit Capetown's Khayelitsha Township. Today, such tours are commonplace.

Most of the families we saw in these communities were by our standards, poorer than poor. Their incomes averaged little more than $100, annually. To our utter amazement however, they were cheerful and friendly. Despite living in flimsy shanties with dirt floors, their barefoot children, meticulously dressed in their one school uniform, acted no differently than children at home.

Shockingly, these are not war-torn countries, where living conditions are unimaginably worse.

These exposures have taught us to never take for granted, our own good fortune, health, and lifestyle, and to share the bounty whenever we can. Our travels have definitely helped us grow as human beings. We are very grateful to have seen some of the worst, as well as the best, in our travels.

....

A caution regarding generosity. Particularly during long-stay vacations, we tend to build up a camaraderie with many of those lucky to be employed in the tourism sector; industrious individuals such as newspaper sellers and beach vendors. We exchange language lessons, leave hats for some who covet ours, buy trinkets we truly do not covet from others, and tend to over-tip.

While our efforts are well-intentioned, we often worry that we may be creating misperceptions and perhaps unfair expectations among these wonderful locals, toward North Americans generally. In the eyes of these hard-working, underpaid people with large families to support, we, lolling in our beach chairs, are all seen as ultra-wealthy.

This is obviously not true of many visitors—in particular those who are really stretching their budget to afford their brief holiday. Not everyone can assist the local economy and its citizens equally.

But everyone *can* deal with their host communities respectfully, and with reasonable generosity.

In many vacation locales world-wide, negotiation on the purchase of goods and services is expected—indeed it is part of the culture. It is important however, that visitors not go overboard in "grinding" these folks down to the lowest possible peso or drachma.

We always try to ensure that such negotiations conclude with both parties satisfied, and smiling. I confess that on occasion, when I did not sense this mutual comfort, I have manufactured a reason to return to the vendor, and have purchased a second item for some-what more than we had previously agreed. When I do that, I almost always get a smile and a handshake, and end up feeling much better. I am at a loss however, how to explain to my wife, my accumulation of unnecessary souvenirs.

....

Many of our memorable travel experiences in other cultures have been almost slapstick. The few adventures that follow are from business-related travels with friend and colleague, Jack.

In a public men's room in South Korea, we were taking care of business at the urinals. A tiny woman suddenly appeared from no-where, mop in hand. She efficiently set to work mopping the floor between our legs as we, trying desperately to be invisible and non-chalant, attempted to finish our task!

....

On another occasion, again in South Korea, we found ourselves with three hours to kill before a scheduled business dinner. Notic-ing a barber-shop pole across the street from our hotel, we both de-cided to get a haircut.

We found it intriguing that we had to first ring a doorbell. We were greeted by a striking young woman, dressed-to-the-nines, who invited us in. Since no one spoke English, we did our best to pantomime that we wanted a haircut.

We were led to a room with two large barber chairs, each facing a sink. After seating us, two young ladies reclined the chairs to the horizontal, removed our shoes and socks, placed a smooth board under our legs, and set our bare feet in the sink. After rolling up our pant legs, each girl took quite some time in washing and massaging our feet.

While this was going on, two other young ladies joined us, to slowly and methodically manicure our hands. When this was all finished, they cleaned our ears with special swabs.

More than an hour had now elapsed, and still no sign of our haircut!

Next came the facial, and the body massage! But it was a massage unlike any I had ever experienced. Instead of using their hands, these petite girls climbed on top of us, and proceeded to massage with their knees, while crawling along our prone bodies! Just when we thought they had completed the task, they had us roll over on our stomachs, then repeated the exercise along our back sides!

Belatedly, I had the presence of mind to point out to Jack that if this were to go on much longer, it would probably cost us $100 each. Not only that, but with still unkempt hair, we would be late for our dinner appointment. Doing our best with sign language, we indicated our need to speed up the procedure.

Finally! Two men, the first males we had seen, arrived with scissors and clippers. They wasted no time. The haircuts were completed in less than ten minutes.

We leapt up, stumbled into our socks and shoes and, in a very mellow mood, were led to the front desk to await our bill. We were flabbergasted! The total cost for the two of us, when translated to dollars, worked out to about $15!

the naked traveller

We subsequently learned that all men's haircuts follow this same ritual. No wonder Korean men are always immaculately groomed! I never did determine whether the ritual in women's salons is similar.

....

In the industrial city of Kobe, in Japan, our hosts took us to a ryokan, a traditional guesthouse, for what they promised would be a relaxing spa session, followed by dinner.

No sooner had we arrived, than we were seated, cross-legged on cushions around a very low table, and served warm sake by four geishas—all quite mature, I might add.

Before long, we were invited to stand up and disrobe. Once we were all in our birthday suits, the geishas took our clothes, handed us dressing gowns, and led us to the bathing room. There, we again disrobed, to climb first into a tub of scalding hot water, followed by a quicker plunge into a tub of shocking ice-cold water.

After switching back and forth several times between the tubs, we were led by our hosts, on all fours, into an adjoining igloo-type steam room, which barely accommodated the four of us as we reclined on bamboo mats and pillows.

Some time later, wiping the steam from our eye-glasses, we emerged once again to repeat the tub ritual. This time we were served refreshing ice-cold sake, while in the hot tub.

Eventually, with great lassitude, we dried off, assisted by the geishas. They handed us our robes, and led us back to the dining room. We again sat on cushions at the low table, and enjoyed a lengthy, delicious Japanese meal.

At the end of the evening, the geishas returned our clothes. We dressed, and were returned to our hotel, pleased to have added yet another unique experience to our repertoire.

peter dolezal

We really do have a lot to learn in North America, about how best to conduct business!

....

In the early 1990's, shortly after the fall of the Iron Curtain, Gaye and I made the first, of what was to become almost annual, visits to eastern Europe.

Early in the days of private enterprise in the former eastern-block countries, a two-tier pricing system was the norm for tourist attractions and accommodations. The lower price, written in words rather than numerals, ensured that most tourists could not understand them. The other, much higher price, was posted in numbers, easily understood by foreign visitors.

On one occasion, the only accommodation available near our hiking destination was in a rather primitive mountain lodge, formerly reserved for vacationing communist officials. Being fluent in the local language, I immediately noticed the dual-pricing system and cautioned Gaye to not speak. Ever budget-conscious, I was determined to arrange our stay at the lower rate.

We were shown to our "deluxe" room with its two single beds, bare ceiling bulb and miniscule sink! The toilet was down the hall, and the shower on a lower level, accessible only through the kitchen! I would give the place a half-star rating, at best!

Each morning Gaye made do with cold sponge baths. I, en route to my shower, waltzed in my nightshirt through the kitchen area, bidding "good morning" to the amazed ladies preparing food! All showered and shaved, I would retrace my steps, once again through the kitchen.

Breakfast and dinner were included in our daily rate. Our meals were silent, lest Gaye's English give away our true status as foreigners. Once in a while she forgot, and I "gently" nudged her foot under the table.

the naked traveller

On our final morning we were seated, awaiting our usual bread, cheese and tea breakfast. Gaye received the usual fare, but added to my selection was a hard-boiled egg.

To this day I am still trying to convince her that it was my incredible charm that earned me the extra treat, and not the fact that the server felt sorry for me, having to care for my silent deaf-mute wife.

For the local population, the posted daily rate for our room and two meals was the equivalent of $6. For foreigners, it was doubled, to a whopping $12!

The lesson in this is that one can, *occasionally*, go too far in stretching the travel-dollar!

....

On our early visits to my Czech roots, we were frequent guests at family dinners. With fork in left hand, and knife in right, I enthusiastically dug into the long-ago flavours of my childhood—roast duck, pig knuckles, and bread dumplings. Gaye, ever polite, cut with her right hand, laid down the knife, shifted fork from left to right hand, placed her left hand in her lap, took a bite, then repeated the procedure until her plate was empty.

Our hostess, my then 83-year old great-aunt, became very concerned. After observing Gaye's strange North American eating habit, she finally asked, "Is there a problem with Gaye's arm? Perhaps we should be serving food that does not require cutting?"

In my role as translator for Gaye, I explained to my aunt, who was not well-travelled, that traditions, including table manners, vary greatly the world over.

....

Fried grasshoppers...sauteed cod cheeks...tripe soup. Food for

the gods for some; for others, it's "I wouldn't touch it if it were served on a silver platter".

Unique to each culture is its diet. The staple, the local starch, whether potato, rice, taro, yam, or other, varies little. What makes the resulting cuisine so different and interesting are the protein sources, the use of local herbs and spices, and the methods of preparation.

Tasting new-to-you foods is an integral part of the travel experience. You may be glad you tried only the tiniest bite. You may, on the other hand, be delighted with your "find", and beg for the recipe.

Snapshots from our travels:

- *In China, a "rat" restaurant which we politely but firmly refused to try.*
- *14 of us sitting down to a 104-dish feast in South Korea.*
- *Tender musk-ox in Canada's far north.*
- *Alligator kebab in Florida.*
- *Roast horse meat in eastern Europe.*
- *Purple pumpkin soup on Australia's Gold Coast.*
- *Piranha appetizers in the Amazon.*

But I still cannot choke down peanut butter at home!

TIP # 58 ...... **Expect to run into cultural differences. Be prepared to adapt to them, learn from them, and consider them a unique, special part of your travel experience.**

CHAPTER TWENTY-SIX

CURRENCY ISSUES

Pounds...Pesos...Rand...Korunas...Yuan...and now...Euros.

Today it is easier than ever to deal with currency-exchange issues. As with most travel details, there are always many ways of approaching the task, some much more beneficial than others.

Gone for the most part, are the days of having to pre-order foreign currency, at very high cost from your bank, simply to get you started at your destination. With the odd exception, this is now unnecessary.

A small float in U.S. dollars, which are accepted world-wide, is always a smart start for your travels. Canadian currency, more difficult, if not impossible to exchange, usually attracts a very poor exchange rate.

Leaving home with about $100 in U.S. small-denomination bills, eases the pressure of having to exchange currency or withdraw funds, immediately upon arrival in a foreign country. *We now make this a regular practice for all our travels.*

Every airport or train station of any size will, in today's world of electronic wizardry, have ATM's which accept international debit and credit cards. Once through *Customs and Immigration*, you can generally locate a machine from which to withdraw local currency.

If you are a frequent *return* visitor to a specific locale, you might plan to return home with enough of that local currency to jump-start your next visit. Tired and travel-worn, you will be happy to avoid having to haul your luggage around the airport or train station, searching for an, at times elusive, ATM.

> **TIP # 59.....The service charge for your cash withdrawal is the same whether you withdraw $20 worth of local currency, or $500. Withdraw sufficient funds to minimize the effect of the service charge.**

Aside from the convenience of around-the-clock instant cash in local currency, the advantage of using an ATM is that you will tend to receive the current, best-possible exchange rate - a far better rate than had you pre-ordered currency from your bank at home.

Even after factoring in the usual $5 withdrawal fee, we find that we routinely receive, at minimum, a 3% better exchange rate, than at a local bank. Not only is the value better, but also, by avoiding the face-to-face teller solution, we avoid long lineups, language issues, and "bankers' hours".

Compare the costs of obtaining local currency through ATMs and even banks, to the much higher rates charged at privately-run Currency-Exchange kiosks, also known as "Weschsel" or "Cambios". The difference can soar to as high as 10%.

....

When using a *credit card*, as opposed to your debit card, to withdraw cash from an ATM, keep in mind that you are *borrowing* money from your card provider. This may be the case even in those instances, when you have a pre-paid credit balance in your account. This is because the computer is often programmed to recognize any cash withdrawal as a "loan". It may take several days before the "loan" is neutralized by your positive balance. In the meantime you may be charged interest. The interest charges begin the day you withdraw the cash—often at rates approaching 30% annually!

The interest will not amount to much *if* you repay the full amount as soon as you arrive home, or even sooner, if you have access to on-line banking. Otherwise, what you have saved with your lower exchange rate, may have evaporated as a result of the much higher penalty in borrowing costs.

To avoid this undesirable situation, try using your **debit card** instead. Have your credit card only as backup in the event the ATM fails to recognize your debit card.

....

Being stranded without access to funds, is a hair-raising experience that with forethought, can be avoided.

If you do not have a regular pattern of foreign travel, consider as well, notifying your credit card company of your planned trip. This pre-empts the risk of a computer-generated "hold" being placed on your card. If the computer senses a major spending-pattern change, it may red-flag your account, suspecting misuse of your card by another party. You may find you are denied its use until you contact the credit card issuer to update them on your location.

TIP # 60.....Whether you withdraw your cash from an ATM using a debit or a credit card, be sure to keep the bulk of your cash in a well-hidden money belt or other pickpocket-proof pocket or pouch. Carry only your *walking-around* cash in a more accessible zippered or buttoned pocket.

Dressed in "tourist" mode, with camera hanging on your neck, you have already identified yourself as a potential target for pickpockets and purse snatchers, many of whom make it their priority to observe ATM activity.

Try your best to avoid ATM's on bustling, high-traffic pedestrian thoroughfares. Much less risky are ATM's located inside the outer doors of most banks. Bright lighting and highly visible security guards, often stationed there, greatly diminish your risk.

Once you complete your withdrawal, make sure your cash, along with your card and printed receipt, are carefully ensconced on your person, *before* leaving the premises. Stuffing your wallet with cash, as you walk out the bank's door, is akin to issuing an open invitation to an unwelcome fleet-footed visitor!

Gaye and I make it a practice to never carry a purse or wallet on our person. A credit card and a day's cash, well-hidden in an inside or secret pocket, along with a photocopy of our key passport page, is all that we generally carry. As much as we prefer not to, losing these items would not ruin our holiday.

TIP # 61..... When travelling, the use of ATM's is safe and economically-sound. Resort only in dire necessity, to on-street currency-exchange kiosks.

....

There was a time when carrying ***traveller's cheques*** was the only way to travel. Some travellers still prefer to use them exclusively. The greatest advantage of traveller's cheques is their loss-protection feature.

Be forewarned however! It is *not* always an easy or straightforward exercise to convert them to local currency.

Friends once arrived in a small remote town one Friday evening with their travellers' cheques, only to discover that no stores would cash them, and the banks would not reopen until Monday.

In some destinations, the local bank is the only place where you can exchange traveller's cheques. This can be a distinct disadvantage when funds are needed after banking hours. Be aware also, that many banks and businesses throughout the world, now charge a hefty fee to exchange traveller's cheques.

In a German bank some years ago, we tried to exchange a $50 *traveller's cheque for local currency. The teller was willing to do so, but at a jaw-dropping charge of ten euros (about $15) for the transaction!*

We have long since tended to avoid traveller's cheques, preferring ATM's as a flexible, 24-hour, good-value currency-exchange option. We take them only if specifically advised to do so by a knowledgeable source, prior to our departure.

....

CHAPTER TWENTY-SEVEN

HEALTH ISSUES

Montezuma's Revenge...Flu pandemics...Malaria...Pneumonia...Yellow Fever.

It is to *your* benefit to be mindful of health issues when travelling, but not to the point of paranoia, which restricts travel unreasonably.

Reasonable health-wise considerations, before booking your trip, include:

- If you have any personal health concerns, check with your doctor, to determine whether your proposed trip poses undue medical risk.

- Use the web to research medical travel-advisories for your destination. A particularly useful site to google is *IAMAT*—International Association for Medical Assistance to Travellers.

- Check well in advance, with your doctor or local travel-health clinic, to obtain information on all advisable or mandatory vaccinations or boosters. Since these vaccinations are seldom covered by your health insurance plans, they must be considered a necessary part of your travel budget.

  Aside from the health protection you receive from appropriate vaccinations before travelling, failure to prove that you are protected, may cause you, upon arrival at your destination, to be refused entry. Carry an updated copy of your official vaccination record with you.

  Travelling without proof of Yellow Fever immunization for instance, can deny you entry into certain high-risk areas of

Africa and South America.

- Ensure that you qualify for out-of-country medical insurance. **Regardless of cost, purchase it for the entire period you plan to be away.** More than just your vacation budget can be destroyed by the lack of medical insurance, should a medical emergency actually occur.

- Carry *all* medications you require during your trip, in their original containers, to ensure no issues arise at border crossings. It is advisable as well, to carry a photocopy of each prescription. Always keep your medication in your hand-carry luggage, to minimize the risk of loss. Carry enough medication to last you in the event that your trip is unexpectedly prolonged.

- If you have mobility or other disability issues, ensure that the vacation you are planning will present no insurmountable challenges.

Having travelled as extensively as we have, we have managed to avoid major problems by following these simple rules. We certainly know of others who, unaware of these precautions, or having chosen to ignore them, have experienced serious difficulties.

Yes, we too have encountered our share of distressing illnesses during our travels, including flu, red eye, food poisoning, sprains and even shingles. Some of these were merely a brief inconvenience; others were severe enough to require a visit to a hospital emergency department, or medical clinic.

Some of these treatments became quite expensive. But since we had all the necessary insurance and documentation, we have always been fully reimbursed on our return home.

TIP # 62.... Simple precautions *before* departure will minimize health and financial risks, and provide peace of mind as you enjoy your travels.

CHAPTER TWENTY-EIGHT

LANGUAGE ISSUES

Habla ingles? Parlez-vous anglais? Mluvite anglicky?

Many less-experienced adventurers are fearful of travelling independently, without the comfort and security of organized tours. The source of their discomfort? Their ability to communicate, should they find themselves in a setting where English is a foreign language.

In most cases, such concerns are unfounded. In today's global economy, English is *the* international language of commerce and tourism. Not only is it taught in most schools, but also, to a much higher degree of fluency, than we are used to seeing in North American schools which teach a second language.

When travelling in Europe, particularly in the larger urban centres, it truly is rare to encounter anyone in the hospitality sector who does not have at least a rudimentary knowledge of English. It can in fact, be downright humbling to encounter so many people who are effortlessly fluent in four or five languages.

As a general rule, we North Americans have become spoiled, with little real need to learn other languages. With only English, a bit of sign language, and a few pantomime skills, you will rarely fail to communicate adequately.

But...should you happen to have some basic knowledge of French, German, or Spanish, you will manage very well in Europe, South America, and much of South-East Asia, even in remote areas.

If you *do* have knowledge of another language, even if only a few words or phrases, don't be shy. Try it out. The local residents may smile, but will fully appreciate your effort, and will respond in kind. Often you will receive a nicer room, or three pears rather than the two you requested—a boon to your budget!

My wife and I are by no means fluent in French, but we can make ourselves reasonably well understood. We once spent two weeks, some 30 kilometers outside Paris, in a charming small village by the name of Brie Comte-Robert. Yes, the local Brie cheese is out-of-this-world!

In the bistros, the library, and the twice-weekly market, we made it a point to communicate in French, even though many of the villagers would have been able, and happy, to converse in English. They were very receptive, polite, and tolerant of our efforts.

One day we chatted for 20 minutes with a retired gentleman who was waiting with us at a bus stop. He spoke not a word of English, but by the time the bus appeared, he had offered to tour us around Versailles the next day! So much for the French reputation of being stand-offish. We have indeed found the opposite to be so.

....

It's inevitable. You *will* eventually encounter the inability to communicate. Don't panic. Innovate!

On a visit to Budapest during the off-season, communication was truly challenging. In one of its magnificent spa facilities, while I was enjoying a massage, Gaye searched for a washroom. Unable to locate one in any of the public areas, she finally encountered a tiny, grey-haired woman mopping the floor in a quiet corridor. Gaye greeted the woman, but was unable to recall a recognizable word for "toilet" among the few Hungarian phrases she had memorized.

The attendant stared blankly, while Gaye tried every foreign word she knew, for "toilet" or "bathroom". Nothing brought forth a reaction. With desperation setting in, Gaye started jumping up and down, crossing her legs. Success! The woman quickly guided her to the elusive washroom. Sign language and theatrics had saved the day—just in time!

Be aware that in asking for a "washroom", you may get exactly that—a room with a sink, but no toilet. The toilet will be in a nearby room.

....

When travelling in more remote areas of some countries, such as China, India, Turkey, or Russia, it may be wise to have a few critical phrases written out in the local language and/or script.

Gaye has a severe sensitivity to garlic. As well as the usual "please" and "thank you", she has memorized the phrase, "I cannot eat garlic", in the local language of every non-English speaking country we've ever visited.

But to be on the safe side, during her month-long volunteer-teaching visit to China, she carried a card with the same phrase written in Chinese characters, by a Chinese-Canadian friend. On the reverse side, another message read, "I am lost. Please direct me to the Tian An Hotel."

....

On arrival at a foreign airport, it is often a good idea to have the name of your hotel along with its address, written out, in case the taxi driver fails to understand your mangled verbal instructions. You may otherwise find yourself cruising around needlessly, as the taxi fare continues to mount.

Miscommunication can occur anywhere, even closer to home. On a local transit bus in a southern Ontario city, the driver told my wife there was no "Pierre" Street on his route. Only minutes later, she caught his attention, pointing out that he had just passed it. The driver admonished her, saying that she had not asked for "Peerie" Street. The spelling had not changed, but the local pronunciation had.

TIP # 63 ..... Don't let the fear of communication deter you. It is usually much easier than you expect; small efforts on your part will be appreciated and usually, understood and reciprocated by locals.

CHAPTER TWENTY-NINE

STAYING IN TOUCH

"Dear Friends: I'm having a marvelous time. I don't know why I didn't hit the road long ago. Wish you were here...."

No matter where on the globe your travels take you, your heart remains at home with family and friends.

In today's techno-world, it is much easier to stay in touch, daily, and even hourly, if you wish. Furthermore, staying in touch has now become very affordable.

In the mid-1990's, as a retirement gift to themselves, our friends set off on a 10-month discovery tour of Europe. Their blended family of six adult children made them promise to stay in touch, at least weekly.

Every Sunday, for 42 weeks, no matter where they were, the search was on for a phone. Often they found themselves squeezed into a booth on a busy street corner, at their pre-arranged calling time. Using their international calling card, they phoned each member of the family.

Over the ten months of their travels, they estimated that those weekly calls cost them a whopping total of approximately $6,000. Aside from the cost of their accommodations, this was the single greatest expense of their entire trip!

Were they to take the same sabbatical today, it would be a much different story. They could stay in touch, even daily for ten months, for little more than a few hundred dollars of internet café, or laptop, time.

Nor would they have to pre-arrange specific calling times, a very inconvenient hassle when time differences and travel schedules come into play.

However did we manage before the **Internet**? Communicating online enables both sender and receiver to sign in, and respond, on their own schedules. Photos can be shared and blogs can be updated. Bills can be paid. Business can be conducted. Newspapers from home can be accessed and read. Enroute travel plans can be researched, finalized, and booked.

It is not necessary to add the extra weight of a laptop to your luggage. Internet sites abound worldwide, usually with very reasonable rates, albeit often with computer keyboard configurations that challenge the wits of any touch-typist.

....

For varied reasons, voice-to-voice contact remains important to many of us.

There are several budget-wise ways to achieve this:

- Generally, it is much less expensive to call *from* North America, to an international location, than vice-versa. If your family or friends at home have an international calling plan and, if you plan to stay in one location for an extended period of time, arrange by e-mail, a specific time when *they* can call *you*. You can then schedule your activities around those expected calls.

   For example, our personal telephone plan in Canada permits us to call anywhere-in-the-world for up to 1000 minutes per month, at no extra cost. This gives us the flexibility and freedom to call friends and family wherever they are, as frequently as we wish.

- **Cell-phones** have become for many, one of today's "must-haves". In most countries you can rent or buy an "unlocked" phone and a local SIM card. The cards are not expensive, and usually allow you to call North America for a few cents per minute.

- Your North American mobile phone may well work in Europe or Mexico with a simple change of chip. The roaming charges however, can be as high as several dollars per minute.

- An alternate, inexpensive option is to buy a country-specific *calling card*, available in local convenience stores, tobacconists, and newspaper stands, in whichever country you find yourself. These cards are good for a specific number of overseas minutes. Usually, the more minutes on the card, the greater the value-per-minute. The cards can be used from any phone, be it in your hotel room, a train station, or a phone booth.

As soon as possible upon arrival in a foreign destination, we purchase a phone card, usually for a minimum of 100 minutes of international calling time, specifically for calls to North America. In Mexico, Europe and Australia, we have been able to call Canada regularly, for as little as three or four cents a minute.

- If you do carry a laptop on your travels, google *Skype* before you leave home to learn how you can call, for free, to other *Skype* users. For a few cents per minute, this site will also allow you to place calls to land lines anywhere in the world.

TIP # 64 ...... **Staying in touch with family and friends from anywhere in the world, is daily becoming easier *and* more affordable. Seek out the best local means for such communication, once you reach your destination.**

CHAPTER THIRTY

FINALLY.......!

1. TRAVEL FRUSTRATIONS

If you travel often enough, you *will* encounter unavoidable frustrations. Nothing makes these challenges more difficult than showing your irritation, losing your cool, or generally, approaching the problem in a negative manner. Try instead to take a deep breath. Approach each situation coolly, and constructively. Your objective? To make the absolute best of an unfortunate or awkward situation.

TIP # 65..... Travel with a positive attitude. Be prepared to be educated, entertained, and exhausted. It won't always be smooth sailing, but each moment of travel will add another page to your book of memorable experiences.

---

2. PASSPORTS and VISAS

If your trip involves travel outside North America, check your passport expiry date. If fewer than six months remain, be sure prior to departure, to renew the passport. A number of countries will not permit entry if your passport does not have a minimum of six months validity remaining, as of your date of arrival.

Although a growing number of countries no longer require visas as a condition of entry, there are those that still do. If you are working with a travel agent, you will normally be made aware of any visa requirements. If booking your trip independently, check visa requirements before proceeding with your travel plans.

3. TRAVEL WITH CHILDREN

If you are a grandparent, solo parent, or other authorized individual travelling with a minor outside the child's country of residence, **always** carry a properly signed, and preferably notarized, "Letter of Authority", granting permission from **both** the child's parents or legal guardians, for travel with you. While such a letter is advisable for minors of any age, it becomes particularly critical for extremely young children who cannot be reliably questioned by Immigration authorities.

For assistance with suitable wording of such a letter, a good sample can be found at ***www.voyage.gc.ca/alt/letter.asp***.

If you are the individual accompanying a minor who is not your child, obtain another letter, signed by both parents or legal guardians, authorizing you to approve any necessary medical treatments which the child may require during the trip. Never forget that all-important medical travel insurance for all children travelling with you.

4. EMERGENCY CONTACT

While you hope that it will never be necessary for relatives or colleagues to have to contact you while you are travelling, emergencies can arise. It is wise to ensure that you can be reached while away from home.

Gaye always creates a detailed itinerary and schedule prior to our departure. She distributes a copy to each of our children, our parents and any others who may have occasion to need to contact us. It includes all our known overnight locations and phone numbers. We often travel with our laptop, although we know that in many places, an internet connection remains difficult to access. We use phone numbers as a prudent back-up.

5. CURRENCY EXCHANGE OFFERS

Never, ever, accept currency exchanges from those who approach you on the street. These slick individuals will often try either to short-change you, or give you counterfeit or long-discontinued currency. Stick to the exchange approaches outlined in Chapter 26.

6. SANITATION ISSUES

North America is privileged to have, for the most part, state-of-the-art sanitation facilities. As you travel further and further from home, you will discover that this is not the norm. To ensure continued good health, adopt super-stringent cleanliness practices.

We always travel with packages of "wet wipes" in our luggage. In our daypack, we carry a small bottle of hand-sanitizer; we use it frequently. When possible, we also rinse with an oral antibacterial mouthwash.

7. PACKING DECISIONS

Only one rule applies...pack light. If an item does not serve more than one purpose, leave it at home. If it can't be easily cleaned, leave it at home. If it's valuable, don't pack it. If it's heavy, think twice about taking it.

8. UNDERSTANDING ONLINE "BOOKING ENGINES"

Be aware that online travel agents such as *www.travelocity.com*; *www.orbitz.com*; or *www.expedia.com* are in fact high-volume on-line travel agents. So too, are some vacation packagers. As such, they will charge you a fee for their services. Additionally, they may not provide access to all discount air carriers or hotel chains. Compare their quotes with other sources, including the traditional travel agency in your neighbourhood.

Similarly, travel wholesalers such as ***www.hotels.com*** tend to work mainly with the larger airlines and hotel chains. This may result in your missing out on better values through smaller carriers and accommodation providers.

TIP # 66..... **Do not rely on one website only to meet all of your travel requirements. Check several sites and other booking options to ensure that you achieve best-value.**

---

9. BUYER BEWARE

Travellers love to shop. Value is not a huge issue if you are buying souvenir trinkets and minor gifts. If shopping for high-value items however, such as jewellery or carpets, for example, take extra precautions:

- Deal with a reputable local licensed shop—rather than a street vendor offering "bargains".

- Do not assume that your tour guide is an expert on quality or value. Often, he will receive a substantial commission for each sale in shops that he recommends.

- Obtain a receipt which clearly describes the item, as well as its cost.

- Insist on charging the purchase to a major credit card.

- As soon as you return home, obtain a professional appraisal to confirm actual value. If grossly different to your receipt, notify your credit card company right away, and request an adjustment.

TIP # 67..... By charging high-value purchases to a credit card, you are more likely to be protected from fraudulent misrepresentation and overcharging on a foreign purchase. Most credit card companies will reimburse the difference on a proven, fraudulent overcharge.

---

10. VALUE-ADDED TAX REFUNDS

Many countries allow foreigners who have made significant purchases, to recover the value-added taxes, if the items purchased accompany you, as you leave the country. Be aware of some facts:

- Only select retailers dealing in higher-value merchandise will offer the necessary certified documentation on purchase. This is required in order to claim your refund at a *Tax Refund* kiosk, located in most airports.

- Usually, upon arrival at the airport from which you are departing the country, you must find the specific *Customs* location, and present your certified proof of purchase, for stamped approval. You may be required to show the merchandise. Be sure to check your luggage only *after* you have these necessary approvals.

- With the requisite Customs approval in hand, you must then find the *Tax Refund* desk, often located in the Departures area, in order to receive your cash refund. You will receive less that the actual tax paid, because, as with most services, you are charged a fee.

- Should you either be unable to locate this refund wicket, or not have the time to do so, you can mail your refund claim. Several months later, you should receive a cheque for the discounted balance owing.

TIP # 68..... In many countries, value-added taxes, included in the cost of major items for export, can at times, exceed 20% of the purchase price. These taxes may be substantially recoverable. Familiarize yourself with the rules and procedures which allow such recovery.

POSTSCRIPT

· ·

*Although this book does not pretend to be all-encompassing, it is my hope that these pages of **Tips** and related experiences will assist in making your future travel planning and vacations simpler, more budget-friendly, and more rewarding.*

Websites to which I have referred are those which I have found to be useful starting points for my various searches. You may find others equally informative or even better. Indeed, new sites are being introduced regularly.

Statutes, rules and regulations to which I have alluded can also change. Always check the latest versions before acting on them.

Other than being with our family, there is nothing we have yet found, that is more enlightening, educational and entertaining, than travel.

Travel has taught us to appreciate our own life, in the context of the rest of the world. We have come to realize that, although economic well-being is still very limited for many, that fact does not always mean they are less happy, or enjoy life less, than we do.

We have observed in fact, that in some of the poorest environments, family ties and mutual support are a greater reality, than is often found in wealthier countries.

One of the greatest gifts we can give our family, is to help and encourage their travel.

Not only we, but also our children and grandchildren, can only but benefit from exposure to other peoples and their cultures. Travel builds not only greater tolerance, but also a stronger appreciation of one's own life.

In sharing with you how we have learned to travel smarter, and how to obtain best-value from our vacation dollar, I hope that you will be encouraged to become more active and passionate participants as members of the global travelling community.

May all your travels be as memorable as ours!

Remember ...... Travel smart. Stretch that dollar. Travel as often as you can! It's an exciting, fascinating world which we all share. Don't leave it unexplored!

I welcome your feedback. If you have comments or suggestions from your own travel experiences, please e-mail me at: **peterdolezal@thenakedtraveller.ca.**